LITTLE RIBBON
PATCHWORK
AND APPLIQUÉ

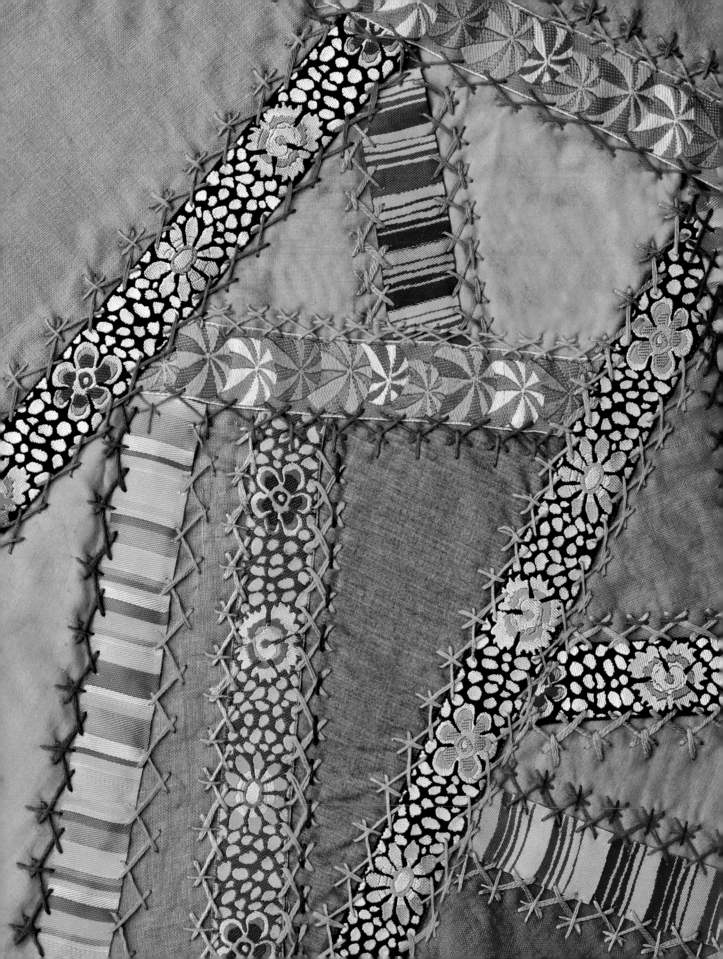

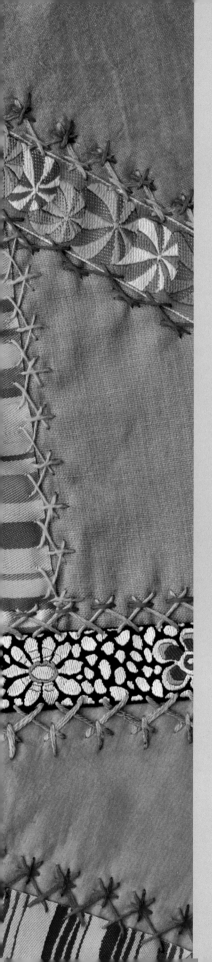

Heart Space Studios

LITTLE RIBBON
PATCHWORK
AND APPLIQUÉ

Colorful designs with
Kaffe Fassett ribbons & fabrics

Photography by Steven Wooster

The Taunton Press

 **The Taunton Press**
Inspiration for hands-on living®

The Taunton Press, Inc.,
63 South Main Street,
PO Box 5506, Newtown, CT
06470-5506
email: tp@taunton.com

First published in the UK in 2015 by
Berry & Co (Publishing) Ltd
47 Crewys Road
Childs Hill
London NW2 2AU

Designer **Steven Wooster**
Editors **Emily Anderson**, **Katie Hardwicke**
Technical editor **Katy Denny**
Stylist **Susan Berry**
Project designs and illustrations **Janet Haigh**

A catalog record for this book is available from the United States Library of Congress.
ISBN: 978-1-63186-260-1

Reproduced in the UK
Printed in China

contents

FOREWORD

Ribbons can be plain, in solid colors or simply striped, or, as in this case, a miniature world of colorful patterns.

I've always loved creating these jewel-like designs, finding graphic shapes that can be simplified enough to read from a width of ribbon. They are a challenge to design because I am limited to just six colors, so when I get it right, the satisfaction is immense—like the the patchwork fabrics I produce, they are meant to be a paintbox of exciting possibilities for creative stitchers.

Janet Haigh of **Heart Space Studios**, with her incisive creative eye, has combined these worlds into a single universe of harmonious colors. With each of her combinations she creates a dance in so many differing moods that I defy anyone not to find one to their taste.

I have tried often to create layouts to show off my own ribbon designs but have never conceived a fraction of the concepts featured in this powerful little book!

Kaffe Fassett 2015

INTRODUCTION

"Made by Hand, Heart & Eye" is the working motto of Heart Space Studios, which was opened in 2011 in Bristol, England, by Janet Haigh, a noted embroiderer and former university teacher of textile design. In a time of mass production and the corresponding loss of craft skills, making by hand is becoming recognized as a sign of both time taken and care given; the maker is producing a gift either for themselves or someone they care about. The aim of the Studios, which has its own shop and gallery, is to inspire people (from complete novices to master crafts people) to try out different materials and learn new skills in the process through workshops and classes run by a group of like-minded crafts practitioners, who disseminate their ideas through exhibitions.

When Kaffe Fassett's delicious ribbons were shown to Heart Space Studios by a colleague, it became immediately obvious that they called out for ways to include them in some new textile designs: students and staff alike have smiled, picked them up, and started to play with them. All textile lovers will find the ribbons fascinating—something about the small-scale perfection of the colors and patterns, and the quality of the weave, whets the desire to work with them.

So we have developed in this book a series of ribbon-inspired patchwork samples based loosely on traditional patchwork patterns and shown how to create them. For some of the samples, we designed a special pieced ribbon fabric that is easily stitched by machine and then patchworked, appliquéd, or embroidered together with other fabrics. The ribbons are also a decorative way to join pieced fabrics instead of using seams (for example, over the seams of crazy patchwork—a real favorite at the Studios), sometimes further embellished with hand stitches. Another idea we had was to turn the ribbons into small, individual yo-yos that led to many different applications, and then further embellish them with buttons, beads, and shisha mirrors.

As the ribbons have woven edges they need very little finishing and the resulting fabrics are firm and pliable; if backed and stitched by machine they are strong and serviceable. They will be useful for numerous small-scale items such as bags, cushions, and lampshades, and even the samples themselves when box framed will look lively on a wall.

The shop and workshop
BELOW At Heart Space Studios, we have both a workshop where we run classes and a shop (below) where members of our design staff can sell their own work to the public.

We have designed a range of projects where the initial samples have been applied to easily sourced bought items, and also created some little handmade projects, including an inventive way to use up any leftover pieces of ribbon for stunning jewelry.

To enable you to make successful ribbon and fabric color choices, it helps to choose one particular woven Jacquard ribbon as the starting point for each design and to use the colors in this to create a set of either harmonizing or contrasting Jacquard, striped, tartan, and plain ribbons and fabrics around it.

The narrow tartan ribbons are really useful for applying to the wider plain grosgrain ribbons to link bands of strong colors in ribbon-fabric designs (see pages 24-29).

We hope this colorful book inspires you to go forward with your own designs, and, following in Heart Space Studios' footsteps, develop your own hand, heart, and eye in the process.

The raw materials

RIGHT The glorious woven ribbons, in mouth-watering colors, that inspired the patchwork design samples and projects in this book.

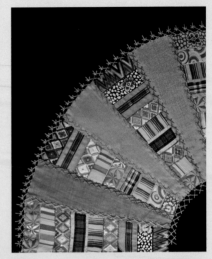

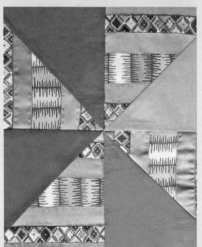

creating ribbon patchworks

This section explains how to make a range of small ribbon patchwork designs using either ribbons alone or ribbons and fabrics combined in various patchwork blocks: in strips, in circles (yo-yos), in irregular crazy forms, and in squares. It also provides some basic know-how for working with ribbons in particular and instructions for the hand embroidery stitches used in the designs. In the second section of the book on pages 92–123, many of these ribbon patchwork designs are translated into finished projects, either applied to bought items or as stand-alone pieces.

Ribbon patchwork essentials

Ribbons

The ribbons are the starting point for all the designs in this book. To create the ribbon patchworks, patterned Jacquard ribbons have been combined with brilliantly colored plain grosgrain ribbons and traditional lightweight woven tartan or checked ribbons (often used as appliqués on wider ribbons) to enhance the overall effect.

To construct the ribbon fabrics and finished projects, you will need a selection of ribbon types and widths, including:

- Woven Jacquard or striped ribbons: $7/8$in (2.2cm) and $1\frac{1}{2}$in (4cm) widths.
- Plain grosgrain ribbons: $\frac{1}{2}$in (1.2mm), 1in (2.5cm), and $1\frac{1}{2}$in (4cm) widths.
- Tartan or checked ribbons: $\frac{1}{2}$in (1.2mm), $\frac{3}{4}$in (2cm), and 1in (2.5cm) widths.

See page 127 for a list of ribbon stockists.

Backing fabrics

Fabrics and ribbons can be backed either to strengthen them or to appliqué them to a base fabric. Two types of backing are needed:

- Iron-on fusible fabric: a fabric with one adhesive side is used to back both ribbons and lightweight main fabrics. It is available by the yard and in different weights. Only lightweight fusible fabric is used in this book. Fused fabrics can also be hand embroidered without using a stretcher or hoop.
- Iron-on fusible web, such as Bondaweb or HeatnBond: a two-sided adhesive paper available in sheets is used to bond the back of an appliqué shape or ribbon to the base fabric.

Fabrics

The fabrics used throughout the samples and projects are from the Kaffe Fassett range of subtle two-toned woven shot cottons. Shot, or two–toned, cottons—where two slightly different colors of warp and weft threads are woven together—are used either as a background or a contrast to the highly decorative ribbons (opposite). Their nuanced tones help them to blend with the multicolored ribbons in the designs. When using lightweight fabric as a base for appliqué or when combined in patchworks with the heavier ribbon fabrics, you may need to back it first (see below left).

Threads

Several different types of stitching threads are used: standard cotton threads in matching colors for general stitching; a transparent nylon thread called monofilament for stitching colored ribbons together where the colors are so different that the stitching needs to disappear; and stranded cotton embroidery floss for decorative hand-stitching (it can be split into narrower strands when needed).

Embellishments

The design samples in this book also have some decorative embellishments, such as shisha mirrors and different sizes and colors of buttons.

Sewing preparation and equipment

Before you begin, you need a clear space, ideally with good natural light, where you can lay your work flat, assemble it, press it, and admire it! If space is limited, it helps to roll up anything you are working on in a clean sheet of fabric between sessions. The following equipment is essential:

For your work area

- Table, or flat surface, large enough to hold all your materials and also so that you can spread out of ribbon lengths used in your projects.
- Sewing machine with sewing needles of varying lengths and widths.
- Ironing board, steam iron, and pressing cloth; set them up near your work table.

Sewing kit and other equipment

Make sure you keep the following items in a handy work box or basket:

Measuring, marking, and cutting A tape measure and a ruler; water-soluble pen; pencil plus sheets of paper and card; a pair of medium-size dressmaking scissors for cutting; small embroidery scissors.

Stitching Hand-sewing needles; embroidery needles; straight pins with metal heads or flat plastic heads used for patchwork; cotton sewing thread; embroidery flosses; clear monofilament thread.

Fabric backing Iron-on fusible fabric; iron-on fusible web.

Ribbons

RIGHT The principal types of ribbons used in this book are printed woven Jacquards (top five ribbons), solid-colored grosgrains (center three ribbons) and tartans and checks (bottom three ribbons).

Special techniques for ribbons

Working with ribbons requires some special attention when measuring, cutting, and stitching.

MEASURING AND CUTTING

Measure the ribbons carefully, laid out flat on the work table. Woven Jacquard ribbons are very dense and sometimes have long floating threads at the back, so always use very sharp scissors to cut them; make a straight cut, not angled, to reduce fraying.

Preventing fraying

Always cut the ribbons just before use, as some ribbons, particularly heavier Jacquards, fray easily. To prevent this, cut a ½-in (1.2-cm) strip of fusible fabric (see page 12) and apply to the back of the cut end immediately. (You can also apply hair spray lightly to the cut ends to prevent fraying immediately before stitching.)

STITCHING

You can stitch ribbons, either together or to a base fabric, in various ways, by machine or by hand, depending on the specific circumstances. Most of the ribbon fabrics in this book are machine stitched, but some, such as the yo-yos, will need to be hand stitched. Ribbons require care in the stitching process, particularly when combining different weights together.

You can choose to sew ribbons together along their length by hand or machine to create a "ribbon fabric" or apply the ribbons in strips to a base fabric (either fusible fabric or to a light-weight cotton), or create a patchwork of mixed ribbons and colored fabrics. These fabrics can then be used to create a finished project (see pages 92-123 for ideas).

MACHINE STITCHING

There are two forms of machine stitching used in this book:
- Zigzag stitching: used for regular close stitching that shows no fabric between the stitches. Set the sewing machine for button-hole-width stitching—usually the lowest number possible—and use the thickest cotton thread that will fit through your needle. When stitching different colored grounds together, use monofilament thread (see below).
- Top-stitching: used to attach ribbons to a background fabric. Top-stitching ribbons onto a base fabric or another ribbon, using a straight stitch along each edge, can be quicker and neater than a zigzag stitch. Use cotton thread to match the appliqué ribbon and a small straight stitch if using monofilament thread.

Using monofilament thread
This transparent thread almost disappears in the stitching process, as long as you make the smallest viable stitches, particularly when zigzag stitching. Use a matching cotton thread in the bobbin of the machine and monofilament in the spool, as two sets of monofilament make for a very tight tension. Make sure, too, that the bobbin tension is tighter than usual so that the cotton thread does not flick to the surface and spoil the finished appearance.

Machine stitching fabrics together to make ribbon fabric

You can make up a fabric entirely from ribbons [fig 1] but when machine stitching different weights of ribbon together, you employ a slightly different technique [fig 2].

1 Cut all ribbons to the required length and lay them out in the chosen order, right sides up.

2 Choose a matching cotton thread in both the bobbin and the top spool of the sewing machine or, when combining ribbons with very different colors, use monofilament thread in the spool and cotton thread in the bobbin.

3 Align the two ends of the first two ribbons to be stitched and place them together under the machine foot. Using the smallest zigzag stitch width possible, stitch the two ribbons together, holding them so that the ends meet [fig 1]. If stitching different weight ribbons together, line up and stitch in the same way but slightly pull the lighter ribbon as you stitch so it remains the same length as the heavier one [fig 2].

4 Continue to stitch the lengths of ribbon together. When complete, place the ribbon fabric right side down and lightly steam press the back using a pressing cloth.

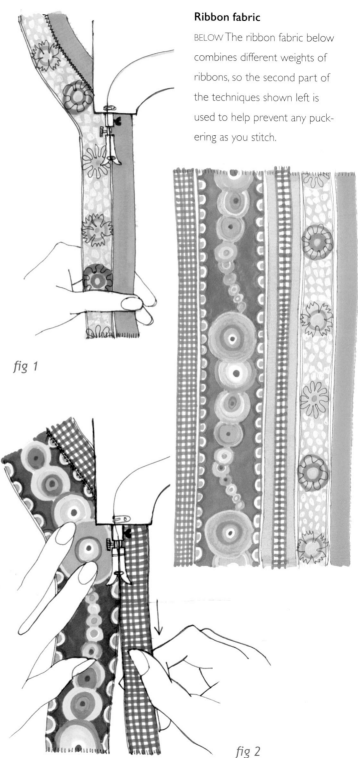

fig 1

fig 2

Ribbon fabric

BELOW The ribbon fabric below combines different weights of ribbons, so the second part of the techniques shown left is used to help prevent any puckering as you stitch.

HAND STITCHING

Hand stitches are used in this book in various ways, either purely for functional purposes (to attach a shisha mirror or a button, for example, as shown right) or to oversew an item where machine stitching is not practical, for example when joining ribbons to make the circular yo-yo shapes (see pages 36-53) or for decoration (see below and opposite).

Simple straight stitches—lines of evenly spaced small stitches—are used for additional decoration in the variations of the basic herringbone stitch, shown opposite.

Running stitches, where small straight stitches are picked up in a group on the needle, are used to gather up the centers of the yo-yos (see page 37).

A little practice on spare pieces of fabric will help you to perfect your hand-stitching technique and allow you to develop a smooth, fluent action.

Decorative hand stitching

There are many decorative stitches you could use but we have limited the range in this book to decorative joining stitches, as they serve a dual purpose: they stitch the ribbons together while adding interesting further texture. The ones shown here are those we like and use frequently but you can incorporate your own stitch preferences in the design samples that follow.

A lampshade project (see pages 112-113) employs a herringbone stitch variation called Cretan stitch, and the instructions for it are given with the project.

SEWING ON BUTTONS AND MIRRORS

These are hand-stitched using strong thread and a suitable needle. Make sure you knot the thread securely to start, and finish with a couple of overstitches at the back of the work.

Shisha mirrors

Hold the mirror in place and oversew around the circumference using small oversewing stitches.

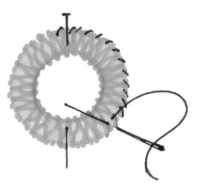

Buttons

Having secured your thread at the back of the work, hold the button in place on the front of it and bring the needle up from the back through the first hole of the button, back through the second hole, and repeat several times before finishing at the back of the work.

Herringbone stitches

Herringbone stitch and its variations are ideal for joining ribbons together or for decorating a ribbon patchwork. The diagrams below show basic herringbone and the simple variations (called tied herringbone stitches used in the ribbon fabrics in this book. There are, in fact, many variations of this attractive yet simple joining stitch, including Cretan stitch (used to join the ribbons on the lampshade, shown on page 113).

Basic herringbone stitch

Work the stitch from left to right as shown, starting the first diagonal stitch at bottom left (A-B) and making the next diagonal from top left to bottom right (C-D). Continue this crisscross pattern across the row.

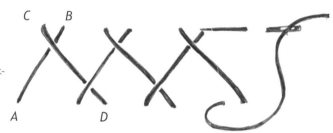

Horizontal straight stitch decoration

Work straight stitches from left to right across the top row of crosses, taking a small straight stitch over each cross. Then work back across the row of crosses beneath from right to left.

Vertical straight stitch decoration

Work vertical straight stitches through the top row of crosses from left to right across the row, then work across the row of crosses beneath from right to left in the same way.

Double straight stitch variation

This version combines both vertical and horizontal straight stitches, working first all the vertical straight stitches before crossing them with the horizontal straight stitches.

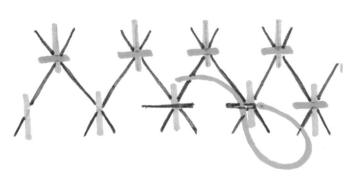

Ribbon strip patchworks

This set of designs features various strip formations composed of ribbons, ribbon fabrics, and fabrics. This simple strip design is composed entirely of plain grosgrain ribbons in different widths and colors, joined with decorative herringbone stitches (see page 17). The ribbons are cut to the same length and laid on a piece of fusible backing fabric. For this particular fabric, bright clear colors were chosen to make a vibrant but light design on which the decorative stitches stand out very clearly.

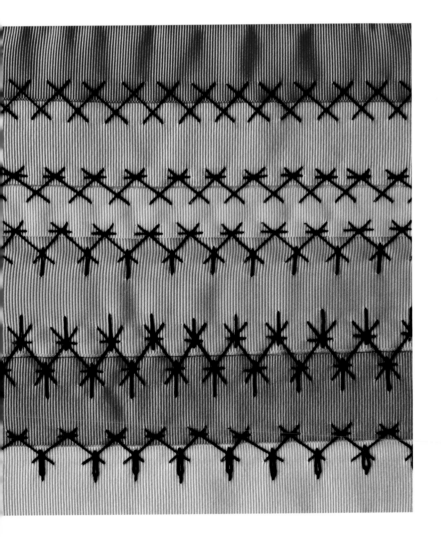

SIZE
6 x 6½in (15 x 16.5cm)

METHOD
Hand stitching

MATERIALS
▶ Four 6½-in (16.5-cm) lengths of 1-in (2.5-cm) wide grosgrain ribbons in three different colors
▶ One 6½-in (16.5-cm) length of 1½-in (3.5-cm) wide grosgrain ribbon in another color
▶ One 6½-in (16.5-cm) length of ¾-in (2cm-) wide grosgrain ribbon in a different color
▶ A 6½-in (16.5-cm) square of fusible fabric
▶ Cotton sewing threads
▶ Stranded embroidery floss or cotton perle thread in a contrast color (black)

How to make

1 Place the piece of fusible fabric shiny-side up. Position the six cut lengths of ribbon in the order shown (right) on top of it. Pin and baste each ribbon to the backing fabric as shown [fig 1]. Remove the pins, and press on the wrong side.

2 Work a row of decorative herringbone stitches (see page 17) over the joins between the ribbons, taking care to catch the edge of each ribbon to the backing fabric as you do so.

3 Remove the basting stitches and turn the work to the wrong side. Press the fusible fabric in place using a steam iron and pressing cloth.

TIP **Adding a border**

To finish off this sample for an appliqué to a cushion, bag or apron, for example, use one of the ribbon colors to create a border around it (as shown on pages 94-95), which will serve to neaten the raw edges of the cut ribbons.

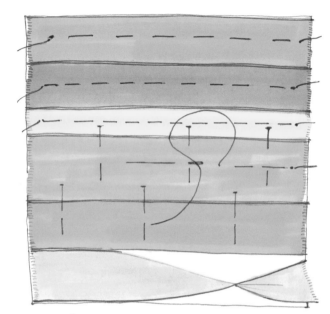

fig 1

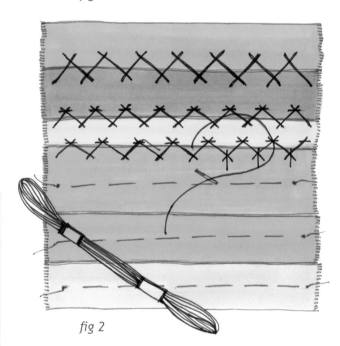

fig 2

Ribbon and fabric strips

This central ribbon strip design is made entirely by hand. The Jacquard ribbons are appliquéd with embroidery stitches onto a fabric backing made up of several harmonizing colored strips, then wider pieces of fabric are placed at each outer edge as borders; the size of the borders can be adjusted to suit the end use (see lampshade project, page 109), making this a very versatile design.

This ribbon fabric uses a mixture of floral Jacquard and striped ribbons, each the same width (in this case, 7⁄8in/2.2cm), that harmonize together, but you could try a version in a mono-chrome palette, using colored embroidery floss to add contrast.

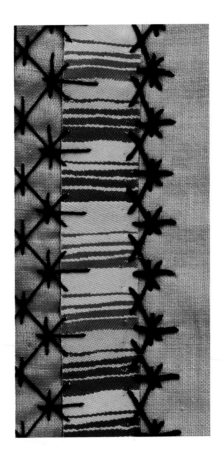

SIZE
10 x 12in (25 x 30cm)

METHOD
Hand stitching

MATERIALS
▶ Four 12-in (30-cm) strips, each 1½in (4cm) wide, of solid cotton fabrics in different colors (to tone with ribbons)
▶ Two wider pieces of solid cotton fabric in two colors, 12 x 3½in (30 x 7.5cm), for borders
▶ A piece of fusible fabric for backing the embroidered section
▶ Three 12-in (30-cm) lengths of 7⁄8-in (2.2-cm) wide striped ribbons
▶ Two 12-in (30-cm) lengths of 7⁄8-in (2.2-cm) wide flower-print Jacquard ribbons
▶ Sewing threads: cottons and/or monofilament
▶ Stranded cotton floss or cotton perle thread in a contrasting color (black)

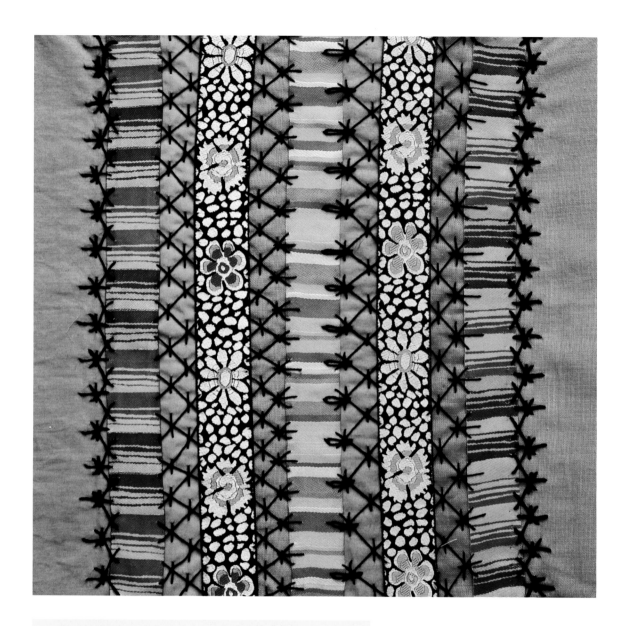

TIP **Machine-stitched alternative**

To make a machine-stitched version of this design, you need to follow the instructions for making ribbon fabric on page 15. If the fabric you use is of lighter weight than the ribbons, you will need to back it with fusible fabric first to prevent the stitching from puckering the fabric as you stitch.

How to make

1 Place the four center strips of fabric onto the fusible fabric, with its shiny-side up, with the larger pieces on the outer edges and the fabric strips between, raw edges aligned [fig 1]. Pin.

2 Arrange the ribbons along the fabric strips, so they cover the fabric joins, with approximately ½-in (1.2-cm) gaps between them to accommodate the embroidery stitches [fig 2]. Pin in place, turn the fabric over, and lightly press the back to bond all the pieces. Remove all the pins.

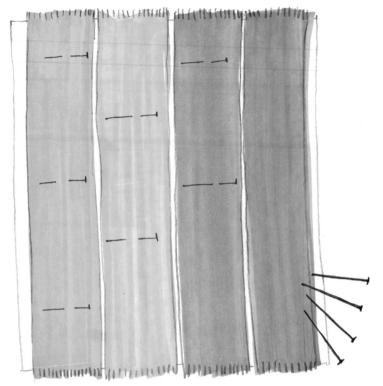

fig 1

TIP **Alternative design**
You can design your own versions of this sample if you take a single brightly colored Jacquard ribbon as the starting point and then look for harmonizing patterned and plain ribbons to go with it. The color match does not need to be precise but it needs to complement it.

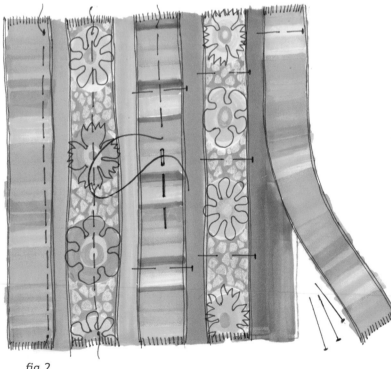

fig 2

3 Working from the central ribbon out, using a variety of herringbone stitches (see page 17) in mirror-image pairs, embroider the ribbons, catching the edges of each adjacent ribbon, and stitching through the backing fabric strips as you do so [fig 3].

4 Attach the far left and far right ribbon edges to the wider edge pieces of solid fabric using more herringbone stitches [fig 4].

5 When complete, press the back of the embroidered fabric lightly with a steam iron and pressing cloth.

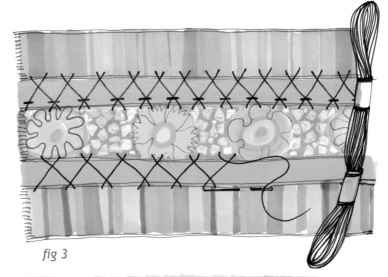

fig 3

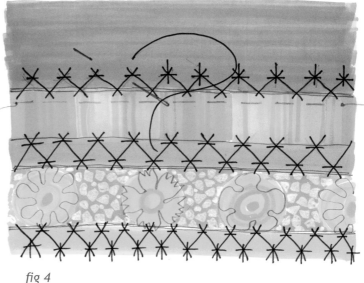

fig 4

ALTERNATIVE CONSTRUCTION
You can easily alter the size of the panel to fit your project by adjusting the width of the fabric strips added to the outer edges of it, and by altering the length of central panel as well. We altered the edge fabric widths for the lampshade on page 109.

Pieced ribbon-fabric strips

This design has been made from premade ribbon fabric (see page 15) in harmonizing shades of blue. It was cut up into four narrow strips, each positioned to ensure that no two adjoining ribbons are the same, an effect inspired by the geometric patchwork of the Seminole Indians. We used the design for a pocket on a plain, brightly colored bag (see page 113).

SIZE
12-in (30-cm) square

METHOD
Machine stitching

MATERIALS
► Ribbon fabric in harmonizing colors, either two pieces 6½ x 13in (16.5 x 33cm), or one piece 13 x 13in (33 x 33cm)
► 12-in (30-cm) square of fusible fabric
► Five 1- x 12-in (2.5- x 30-cm) lengths of fusible fabric
► Five 12-in (30-cm) lengths of 1-in (2.5-cm) wide plain grosgrain ribbon
► Narrow ½-in (1.2-cm) wide tartan ribbon for appliqué (see Step 4 on page 27)
► Machine sewing threads: matching cotton threads and/or monofilament (see page 12)

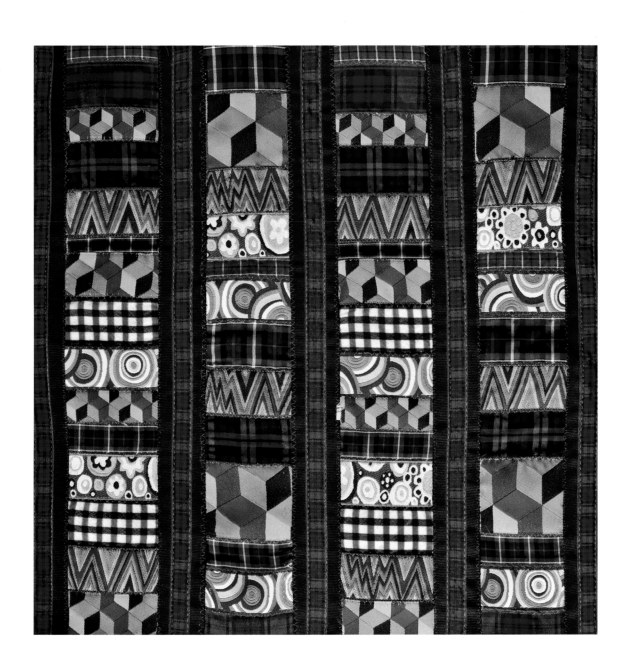

How to make

1 Cut up the ribbon fabric into four pieces of equal length [fig 1].

2 Arrange the strips of ribbon fabric on top of the fusible fabric with its shiny-side up and with the edges of the strips just touching. Position the strips so that they do not repeat the same pattern in neighboring rows. Also, take care not to put strongly patterned ribbons next to one another or they will dominate the whole piece. Pin and baste into position [fig 2].

fig 1

ALTERNATIVE METHOD
You can pin, baste, and stitch the decorative narrow ribbon to the grosgrain ones before Step 3 if you have already decided this effect is required.

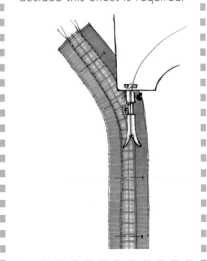

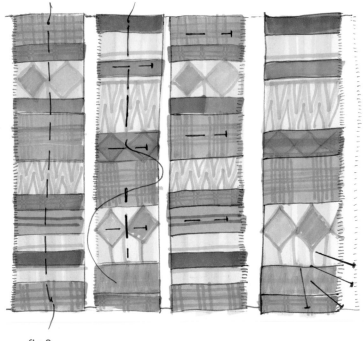

fig 2

3 Back the grosgrain ribbon pieces with lengths of fusible fabric (see page 12). Center the grosgrain ribbon over the joins between the strips of ribbon fabric. Pin and baste into position [fig 3]. Turn the fabric over and lightly press so that all the elements are bonded together.

4 Check that your choice of narrow tartan ribbon for the appliqué matches the color balance of the stitched fabric, and change if necessary. Cut the narrow tartan ribbon to the same length as the grosgrain ribbons. Pin each one to each grosgrain ribbon. Using matching cotton thread, or a monofilament thread, machine-stitch the narrow tartan ribbons at each side [fig 4].

5 Then, using the smallest manageable zigzag stitch, stitch the edges of the grosgrain ribbons to the ribbon fabric strips [fig 5].

6 Remove all pins and basting thread and press the back of the panel with a pressing cloth.

fig 3

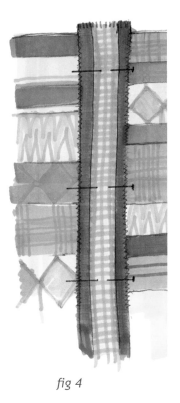

fig 4

fig 5

Flying geese strips

This is a traditional patchwork design block in which triangles of ribbon fabric made from a mix of Jacquard, grosgrain, and tartan ribbons are combined with solid-colored fabric to add zest to the design. Each row of triangles alternates a ribbon fabric piece with a solid fabric. To ensure that the cotton fabric does

SIZE
Approx. 19½ x 9½in (49.5 x 24cm)

METHOD
Machine stitching

MATERIALS
▶ Three 17½ x 3½-in (44.5 x 9-cm) strips of ribbon fabric in a range of Jacquards, grosgrains, and tartans in three distinct colorways—we used greens, blues, and reds
▶ Twelve 5-in (12-cm) solid fabric squares (charms), in colors to harmonize with the ribbon fabrics
▶ Twelve 5-in (12-cm) fusible fabric squares (optional, see above)
▶ Machine sewing threads: matching cotton threads and monofilament
▶ Ribbon triangle template A (see page 127)
▶ Water-soluble marker pen or pencil

not pucker when stitched to the heavier-weight ribbon fabrics, it will need to be reinforced by ironing fusible fabric to the back of each fabric square before it is cut into the triangle shapes. The ribbon acts as a selvedge on the long side of each triangle, whereas the triangles cut from the fabric squares do not have a selvedge, so you need to take care when placing these elements together before stitching them.

How to make

1 Place template A onto the first ribbon-fabric strip with the clipped tip at the top. Align the template so there is little waste, and mark the shape on the ribbon fabric with a water-soluble pen or pencil. Flip the template so that the longest side is at the top, align it with one of the marked sides, and mark in the other side, to give an inverted triangle. Repeat along the strip to give three ribbon triangles [fig 1]. Repeat for the other two ribbon-fabric strips, giving a total of nine ribbon triangles.

fig 1

2 Fold the 12 charms in half diagonally, fingerpress to mark the crease, and cut along the fold. Divide the ribbon-fabric triangles and the charm triangles into their three color groups. Then arrange them into three straight strips made up of seven triangles each—three ribbon triangles and four charms in each strip [fig 2]. Start the strip with a charm, with its longest side at the top, alternating with a ribbon triangle, as shown.

NOTE *The ribbon-fabric triangles have a selvedge on the long side. The charm triangles do not. Therefore, you have to be careful when stitching them together in Step 3 to make an allowance for this difference (see the top of the artwork below).*

fig 2

3 Take the first fabric triangle of one of the strips and flip it over onto the neighboring ribbon triangle along the short, diagonal edges where the two meet, so that the right sides are together. Pin and baste, paying attention to the corner placements so that the tips align [fig 3]. Machine-stitch taking a ¼-in (6-mm) seam. Press the seam allowance toward the cotton fabric.

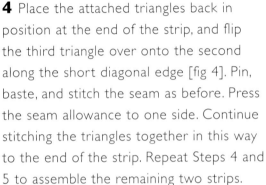

fig 3

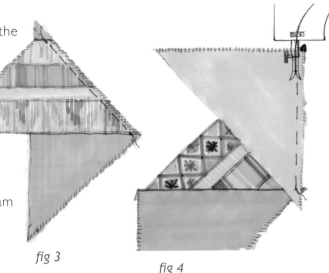

fig 4

4 Place the attached triangles back in position at the end of the strip, and flip the third triangle over onto the second along the short diagonal edge [fig 4]. Pin, baste, and stitch the seam as before. Press the seam allowance to one side. Continue stitching the triangles together in this way to the end of the strip. Repeat Steps 4 and 5 to assemble the remaining two strips.

5 To sew the strips together, position the first strip with the ribbon-fabric triangles pointing upward. Place the next strip above

and overlap the bottom edge so that the apex of the ribbon triangles on the bottom strip sit at the center of the base of the ribbon-fabric triangles above [fig 5]. Top-stitch the bottom edge of the second strip to attach it to the first strip. Repeat to add the final strip, again top-stitching it to the strip below and ensuring the alignment of the triangles is correct. The woven edge of the ribbon triangles covers the raw edge of the solid charms.

fig 5

Embroidered diagonal ribbon-fabric strips

This striking design employs a limited color range to great effect. The ribbon-fabric panel has been hand-embroidered into position and the flowered Jacquard ribbons repeated as borders. With the addition of extra fabric at each outer edge it makes an eye-catching cushion (see page 99) but would also work well on a lampshade (see page 106).

SIZE
Approx. 16-in (40-cm) square

METHOD
Machine stitching and hand embroidery

MATERIALS
► Strip of ribbon fabric measuring 18 x 4½in (45 x 11.5cm)
► 16-in (40-cm) square of furnishing weight solid-colored cotton fabric
► Two 16-in (40-cm) lengths narrow checked ribbon, ½in (1.2cm) wide
► Two 16-in (40-cm) lengths floral Jacquard ribbon, ⅞in (2.2cm) wide
► Machine sewing threads: matching cotton thread and monofilament (see page 12)
► Stranded embroidery floss in a bright color, to contrast with the flowered ribbon
► Triangle template B (see page 127)
► Water-soluble marker pen or pencil

How to make

Making the ribbon triangles

1 Place template B onto the strip of ribbon fabric so that the right-angle corner of the template aligns with the bottom left-hand corner of the ribbon fabric. Mark around the template with a water-soluble pen or pencil [fig 1]. Flip the template over along the long side so that the left edge is now the top edge. Mark again. Continue in this way, top to tail, all along the ribbon-fabric strip, until you have marked 6 triangles, and cut them out. Each resulting triangle will have two raw edges and one finished (woven) edge.

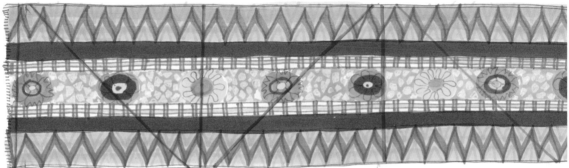

fig 1

2 Arrange the triangles into a straight strip, so that the long edges are at the top or bottom, and each finished short edge overlaps a raw short edge. Pin and baste into position with raw edges of one triangle protruding beyond the selvedge of its adjacent triangle [fig 2]. Then top-stitch the triangles together using monofilament thread with a single straight machine stitch [fig 3].

3 Continue to the end of the row and then steam press the reverse, using a cloth.

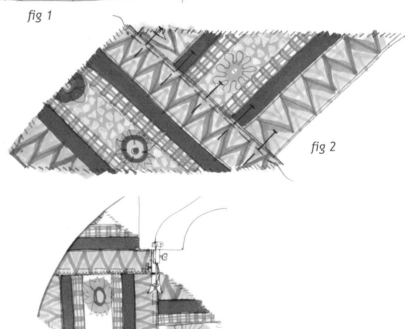

fig 2

fig 3

Adding the ribbon rows

4 Fold the backing fabric in half and mark the crease. Center the strip across the fabric on the crease; pin and baste in position.

5 Position the two lengths of narrow checked ribbon so that they overlap and hide the raw edges of the triangle strip. Top-stitch the ribbons along each edge. Pin and baste the Jacquard ribbon ½–¾in (1.2–2cm) to the outer edges of the checked ribbons (so that a strip of back-ing fabric shows through) [fig 4].

Embroidering the ribbons

6 Work rows of herringbone variations (see page 17) between the two sets of ribbons and the outer edge of the Jacquard rib-bons using strongly contrasting embroidery floss [fig 5].

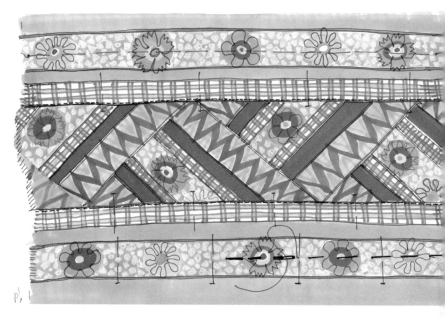

fig 4

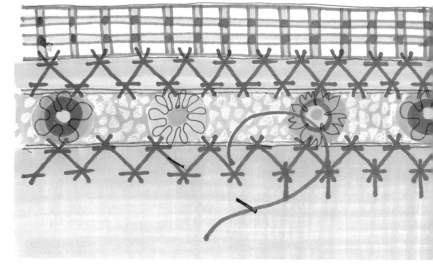

fig 5

TIP **Special attention!**
When stitching the triangles of ribbon fabric together, you need to position them care-fully to allow a turning on the raw edge (where the finished [woven] edge of one triangle is stitched to the raw edge of the adjacent one).

Circular (yo-yo) ribbon patchworks

The patchwork yo-yo designs in this book are inspired by yo-yo patchworks, where small patches of fabric were gathered around a circular template and then joined together. The yo-yo designs in this book feature ribbon and/or ribbon-fabric yo-yos. Single ribbon yo-yos are formed entirely by hand. Double yo-yos can be made from a piece of ribbon fabric that is stitched together by hand or machine (see Making ribbon fabric, page 15). To work a single yo-yo, work only Steps 2 and 3 opposite, using a single wide ribbon.

SIZE
Each single yo-yo measures approx. 2¼in (5.5cm)
Each double yo-yo measures approx. 4in (10cm)

METHOD
Hand stitching

MATERIALS
▶ For a single yo-yo: a 7-in (18-cm) length of 1-in (2.5-cm) wide grosgrain ribbon
▶ For a double yo-yo: two pieces of ⅞-in (2.2-cm) wide Jacquard ribbon, each 12in (30cm) long, in different harmonizing patterns.
▶ 4 small buttons in similar colors
▶ Strong thread

How to make

1 Place the right sides of the two different Jacquard ribbons together, and oversew the edge of each to the other as shown, to create a ribbon-fabric strip [fig 1].

2 With a needle and strong matching thread, secure one end of the thread at one end of the proposed inner edge of the ribbon fabric and work a series of ¼-in (6-mm) long running stitches [fig 2].

3 Gather up the stitches to pull the fabric into a circle. Then run a row of short straight stitches to sew the ends together, and oversew the raw edges to one side to neaten [fig 3].

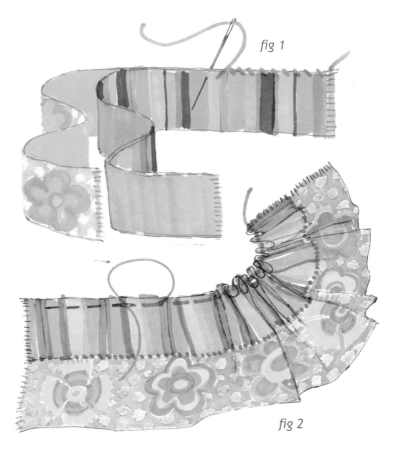

fig 1

fig 2

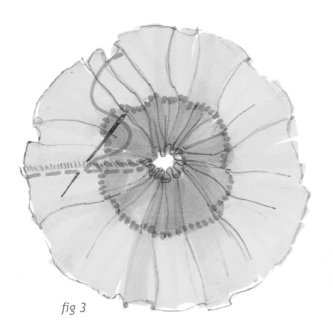

fig 3

TIP Alternative design
You could make any number of single and double yo-yos in harmonizing colorways and stitch them to a piece of backing fabric through the holes of the button. We did this with the lampshade on pages 106-107, but a group of yo-yos, positioned so that their edges just touch, would make an attractive decoration for a store-bought plain cushion cover too.

Embroidered yo-yo blocks

Placing a circle within a square patch is one of the simplest ideas in this book—but by embroidering a double-ribbon yo-yo onto a square of matching fabric, it becomes a rich and varied way of patterning patchwork. Stitching several squares together, and embroidering over the seams in different colorways, as here, adds to the design possibilities. Alternatively, creating the yo-yos from plain ribbons in two different bright colors, placing them on contrasting solid, bright cotton fabrics, and hand-stitching them in a single colored thread (see Alternative crazy patchwork designs on page 59) would give a very different dimension to the design. It would be very easy to add more squares to this design to create a small throw.

SIZE
9½-in (24-cm) square

METHOD
Hand stitching, machine stitching,
hand embroidery

MATERIALS
▶ Four 11-in (28-cm) lengths of ⅞-in (2.2-cm) wide Jacquard ribbon
▶ Four 11-in (28-cm) lengths of ½-in (1.2-cm) wide harmonizing tartan ribbon
▶ Four 5-in (12-cm) squares of solid cotton in colors that harmonize with the ribbons
▶ Four 5-in (12-cm) squares of fusible fabric
▶ Stranded embroidery floss in matching colors
▶ Light-colored marking pencil

How to make

1 Make four double-ribbon yo-yos with one tartan and one Jacquard ribbon for each one (see page 37), using the tartan ribbon for the inner circle.

2 Bond the fusible fabric squares onto the backs of the solid cotton squares. Find the center of the prepared squares (see below), then pin and baste a yo-yo in the center of each one [fig 1].

3 Using the fabric marking pencil, draw a circle approximately 2in (5cm) in diameter onto the backing fabric, so that it is slightly larger than the yo-yo [fig 2].

> **TIP Finding the center of a square**
> Fold the square of fabric in half and run your finger along the fold to make a crease, open out and fold it in half in the opposite direction, and repeat to crease again.
> The center point where the folds meet is now the center of the fabric. Mark with a water-soluble pen.

fig 1

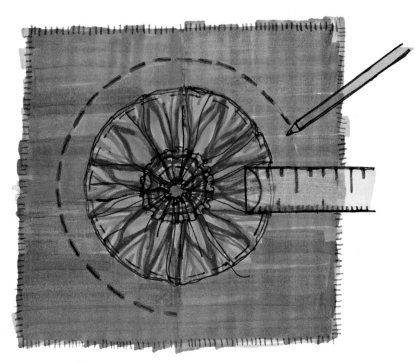

fig 2

4 Using four strands of embroidery floss together, work tied herringbone stitches (see page 17) around the edge of the yo-yo, catching the edge of the ribbon and using the drawn circle as a guide for the outer edge [fig 3].

5 Make three more embroidered yo-yo squares in contrasting colors to the chosen background fabric colors, such as a red ribbon on a blue background or a blue ribbon on a red background.

6 Pin, baste, and stitch the four squares together, alternating the colors, taking a ¼-in (6-mm) seam. Work rows of tied herringbone stitches in a contrasting colored thread over the seam lines [fig 4].

7 Lightly press the back of the fabric when all the stitching is finished.

fig 3

fig 4

Triple ribbon yo-yo

This large, circular triple yo-yo could easily belong to another era—it is reminiscent of crinoline-clad ladies seated on a chintz-covered couch! These woven Jacquard and gros-grain ribbons come in such delicious sugar-almond colors that they just ask to be made into something very feminine.

This fabric is created by hand from three different widths and lengths of ribbon strips that have previously been machine-stitched together (see page 15) to make a strip of ribbon fabric.

We used the design here to make a stuffed boudoir-style cushion on page 102.

SIZE
12½in (31cm) diameter

METHOD
Hand and machine stitching

MATERIALS
▶ Three strips of ribbon fabric, each made up of different widths of Jacquard and grosgrain ribbons:
  Inner strip: 13 x 2in (33 x 5cm)
  Middle strip: 27 x 2in (68.5 x 5cm)
  Outer strip: 41 x 2½in (104 x 6cm)
▶ Strong sewing thread or embroidery floss (such as cotton perle) in colors to blend with ribbon edges
▶ Water-soluble marker pen

How to make

1 Create three strips of machine-stitched ribbon fabric (see page 15) from a mixture of harmonizing plain grosgrain and printed Jacquard ribbons (like the ones shown in fig 1 and fig 2) to the lengths given.

2 Fold one strip in half and mark the center with a water-soluble pen on the edge. Fold again and mark the quarters [fig 2]. Repeat for each strip.

Inner strip

3 Using a matching strong thread, work a row of running stitches along what will become the inside edge of the inner ribbon-fabric strip, and make it into a yo-yo (see page 37). When complete, lay it right side up on a flat surface.

Middle strip

4 Work a row of running stitches along what will become the inside edge of the middle ribbon-fabric strip, and pull the thread to gather the ribbon enough to fit around the outer edge of the yo-yo from Step 3. Pin the edges of the strips together, matching up the quarter markings. Make sure that the end seam does not align with that of the inner yo-yo [fig 3].

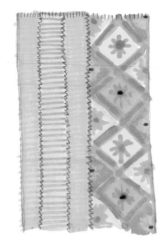

fig 1

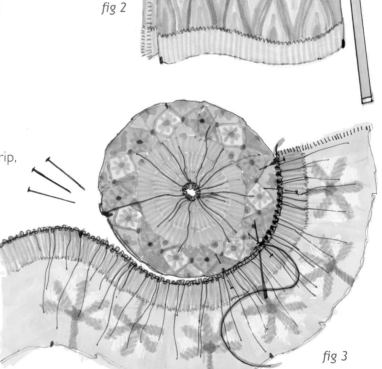

fig 2

fig 3

5 Oversew the ribbon edges together by hand, making sure that the gathering is evenly distributed. When complete, sew up the ribbon-fabric seam.

Outer strip
6 Take the outer ribbon strip and repeat the placement and stitching as for the middle strip [fig 4]. Turn the whole piece over and steam press lightly.

TIP **Alternative method and/or design**
The inner strip of ribbon fabric shown here is made with a narrower strip of contrasting ribbon appliquéd to a wider one (as shown on page 27). Each of the strips of ribbon fabric have been machine stitched but you could, if you prefer, oversew them together by hand, as shown for the double yo-yo on page 37. You could also use other ribbons in different colors for this design, but make sure you match the widths of the ribbons shown in these three pieces and that you keep the lengths the same.

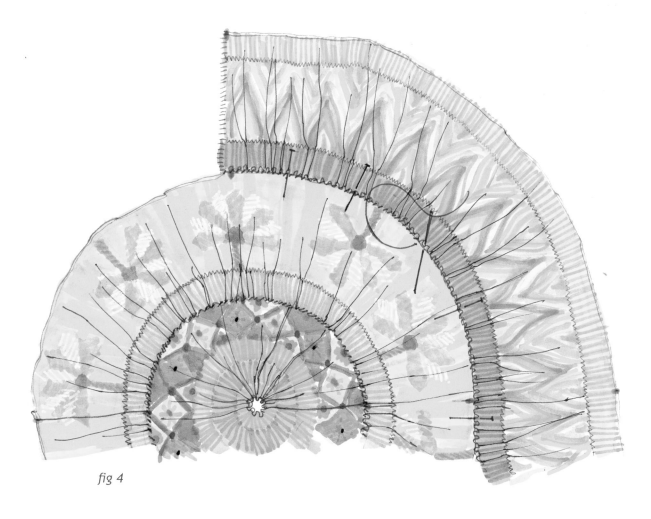

fig 4

Jacquard ribbon yo-yos in strips

This is one of the first inspirational designs we developed for the book. Making the small yo-yos from the beautiful woven Jacquard ribbons and placing them between lines of the same ribbons guarantees that the different elements blend together.

Arranging the yo-yos on strips of harmonizing fabrics makes the whole design richer and more subtle. The yo-yos are stitched to the solid-colored backing fabric, and the ribbons, just touching the edges of the yo-yos, cover the joins between the fabric strips. The finished fabric would make an attractive textured cushion.

SIZE
Approx. 10-in (25-cm) square

METHOD
Hand and machine stitching

MATERIALS
▶ 15 single yo-yos made from ⅞-in (2.2-cm) wide Jacquard and striped ribbons (each yo-yo is 1¾in/4.5cm in diameter and requires 6in/15cm of ribbon), see page 37
▶ Four 11-in (28-cm) lengths of the ⅞-in (2.2-cm) wide Jacquard ribbon
▶ Three strips of plain cotton fabric in different colors (to harmonize with ribbons)
▶ 11-in (28-cm) square of fusible fabric
▶ 15 small, two-hole shell buttons
▶ Machine sewing threads: matching cotton thread and monofilament (see page 12)
▶ Water-soluble marker pen

How to make

1 Place the three strips of fabric on top of the fusible fabric (which is placed shiny-side up) and align the edges so they just meet. Pin to the backing fabric. Measure the yo-yos, or place a couple onto a fabric strip to ascertain the correct position, and then place the ribbon lengths on either side so they will just touch the outer edges of each yo-yo. Pin the ribbon in place [fig 1].

2 Place the other ribbon lengths along the joins of the fabric strips. When all are in position, top-stitch using matching cotton or monofilament thread [fig 2].

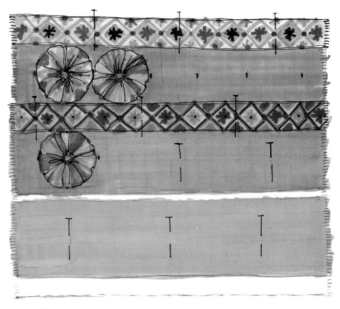

fig 1

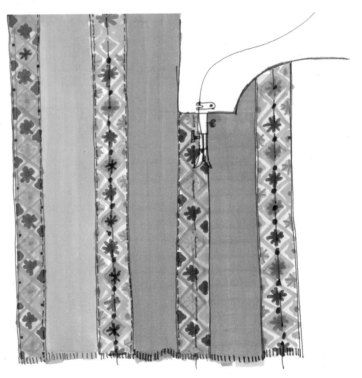

fig 2

TIP **Alternative design**

If you prefer, this design would look both lively and strong using bright contrasting colors for the fabric base and similarly bright contrasting plain grosgrain ribbons in place of the patterned Jacquard ones. The buttons at the center of each yo-yo could also provide a strong contrast.

3 Arrange one row of five yo-yos side by side with no gaps between them [fig 3] onto one of the fabric strips and pin into position. Continue covering the background fabrics with the rows of yo-yos.

4 Sew the buttons to the center of each yo-yo [fig 4]. Attaching them to the background fabric in this way will keep the yo-yos in place.

5 Oversew the edges of the yo-yos by hand onto the ribbon strips [fig 5].

6 When complete, press the back of the embroidered fabric lightly with a steam iron.

fig 3

fig 4

fig 5

Half yo-yo band

The inspiration for creating half yo-yos came from the idea to stitch them to a ribbon band. Stitching the half-circles to other ribbons allows this idea to be developed into many different fabrics that would lend themselves to all sorts of other uses, such as the half yo-yo buttonband decoration for the shirt on page 118. But it would also make an equally good decoration for a lampshade, for example, in a strip around the base and top of the shade, or for a hat band, perhaps. Choosing buttons that harmonize with the ribbons in this design helps to pull the two different colorways of Jacquard ribbons together.

SIZE
8½ x 12in (21.5 x 30cm)

METHOD
Hand and machine stitching

MATERIALS
▶ For each half yo-yo, a 6½-in (16.5-cm) length of 1½-in (4-cm) wide Jacquard ribbon

▶ Five 13-in (33-cm) lengths of ½-in (1.2-cm) wide checked ribbon

▶ Background fabric, 13-in (33-cm) square

▶ Fusible fabric, 13-in (33-cm) square, or same measurement as background fabric

▶ Medium-sized buttons to harmonize with Jacquard ribbons

▶ Strong cotton sewing thread

▶ Machine-sewing threads: matching cotton thread and monofilament (see page 12)

▶ Water-soluble marker pen

How to make

1 Make each half yo-yo by working running stitches along the length of each piece of ribbon and then doubling back again when the shape becomes a horseshoe [fig 1].

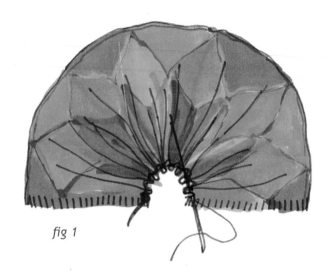

fig 1

2 Mark the center of the background fabric. Draw two horizontal lines, ½in (1.2cm) apart, on either side of the center line. Place one row of half yo-yos edge to edge on the upper line, with the center of one on the center of the fabric, alternating the colors [fig 2]; pin and baste in place.

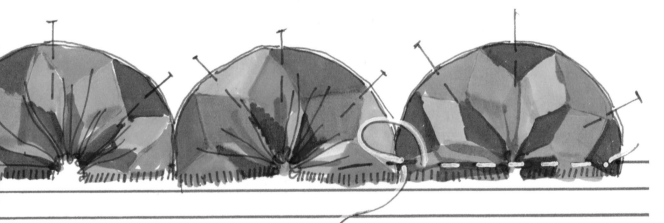

fig 2

3 Place a second row of half yo-yos on the lower marked line as shown at right—the rows about ½in (1.2cm) apart. Pin and baste into position. Then position the first length of checked ribbon over the yo-yo centers, tuck under the ribbon ends [fig 3] and baste in position.

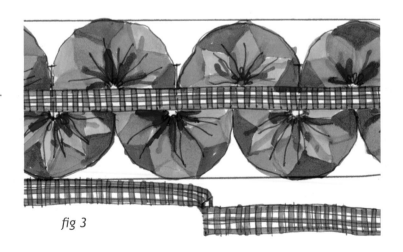

fig 3

4 Place the strips of checked ribbon on either side of the yo-yo edges so they just cover the outermost edges, tuck under the ribbon ends, and baste in position. Machine-stitch the ribbons in position using either monofilament or a matching cotton thread. Use a small zigzag stitch, making sure that the edge of each yo-yo frill is stitched in with the checked ribbon along the top edges [fig 4].

5 Sew a button in place (see page 16) over the central gap in each yo-yo [fig 5], making sure the edge of each button is not covered by the ribbon. Turn the finished piece to the wrong side and press very lightly with a pressing cloth.

TIP **Button detail**
When choosing buttons make sure they are large enough to cover the gathering stitches at the center of the yo-yo. To accentuate the different colors of the yo-yos, you could use a contrasting colored thread for each of the two colorways of the half yo-yos.

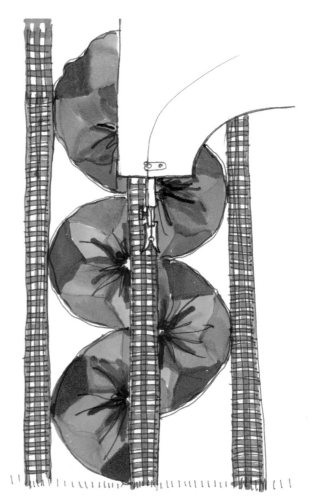

fig 4

fig 5

Crazy ribbon patchworks

Crazy patchwork is an irregular system of piecing in which oddly shaped scraps of fabric in an array of colors are joined together, either by machine stitching or by hand embroidery. In this book we have chosen to cover the joins between the fabric scraps with different types and colors of ribbon, which further enhances the crazy appearance. In the simplest form shown here, the ribbons are machine stitched to the crazy patchwork base fabrics.

SIZE
8 x 7in (20 x 18cm)

METHOD
Machine stitching

MATERIALS
▶ 6 scraps of solid-colored fabric in different colors
▶ 5 scraps of ⅞-in (2.2-cm) wide Jacquard ribbons in harmonizing colors
▶ Piece of backing fabric, 8 x 7in (20 x 18cm)
▶ Monofilament or harmonizing thread

1 Starting in the top left corner, place one scrap of fabric on the backing fabric and pin in position. Position each new scrap of fabric by butting it up to the preceding piece or pieces [fig 1] until you have covered the square, making sure that each piece contrasts with its neighbor. Pin in position. Turn over and press. Remove pins.

2 Place the ribbons over each join, cutting each one to fit. Each new ribbon must cover the raw ends of the preceding ribbons. Pin and baste all into position [fig 2].

3 Using monofilament or matching thread, zigzag stitch into position, using the narrowest possible stitch width [fig 3].

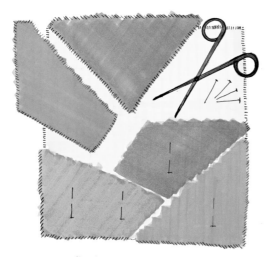

fig 1

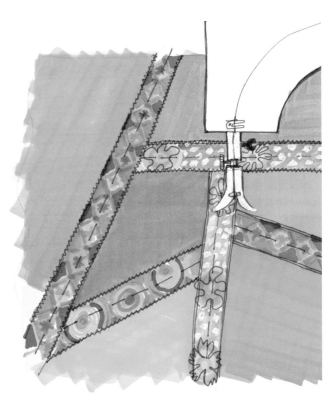

fig 3

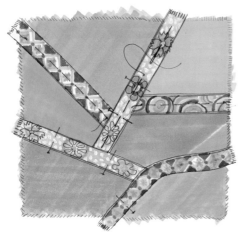

fig 2

Hand-embroidered crazy ribbon patchwork

This design is based on a typical crazy patchwork design but instead of using embroidery stitches alone to hold the patches together, brilliantly colored Jacquard and striped ribbons have been laid over the joins of the fabric patches, hand-embroidered to the fabric over each edge, creating a richly embellished fabric.

To make the embroidery stitches particularly visible, choose colors for the threads that will contrast with the colors of the cotton patches. These contrasting colors—pink on top of blues and/or greens, green on top of rusts and/or reds—will make the color scheme more vibrant.

SIZE
12-in (30-cm) square

METHOD
Hand embroidery

MATERIALS
▶ Six ribbons (two different stripes and four different Jacquards) each ⅞in (2.2cm) wide and approximately ½yd (45cm) long
▶ Scraps of solid-colored cotton in five or six different colors to harmonize with the ribbons
▶ 13-in (33-cm) square of backing fabric
▶ Stranded cotton embroidery floss to match or contrast with the chosen fabrics

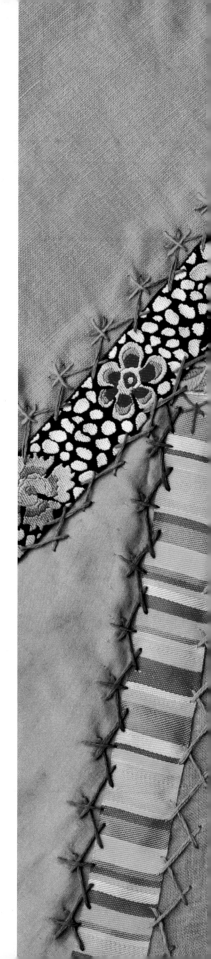

How to make

1 Create the basic crazy fabric base, follow the instructions given on page 55, adapting Steps 1 and 2 to fit your larger square of backing fabric, and using more scraps of fabric as required. Pin the pieces in place [fig 1].

2 Starting at the top left-hand corner, using stitches in a contrasting thread to the color of the background fabric, work a row of foundation herringbone stitches and then work tying straight stitches over them in a variety of colors. Continue to work decorative herringbone stitches in mulitcolored threads to contrast with the base fabrics over all of the ribbon edges [fig 2].

Note As you create the patchwork, you may find you get an occasional gap. You can fill these in quite simply using a piece of matching ribbon and patching it over the gap, taking care to turn over any raw edges to align with the patch where the gap occurred. Stitch as instructed for the rest of the sample.

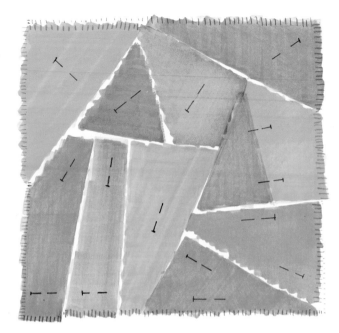

fig 1

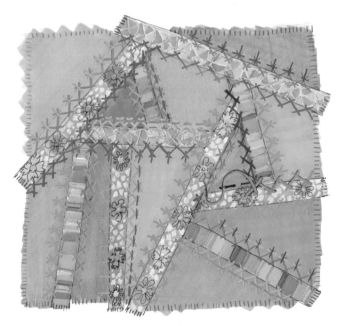

fig 2

Alternative designs

Because crazy patchwork is by nature very irregular, you can choose to create quite strikingly different designs and placements. In the two samples here, we have used solid-colored fabrics and contrasted them with plain grosgrain ribbons in strong contrasting colors.

Sample 1 This design uses five different solid-colored fabrics and five colors of ribbons for the crazy patchwork block and just one contrasting color of embroidery floss in a range of different decorative herringbone stitches.

Sample 2 This design uses six different solid-colored fabrics and ribbons, and six different colors of decorative herringbone stitches, each positioned for maximum contrast with the fabric they cover.

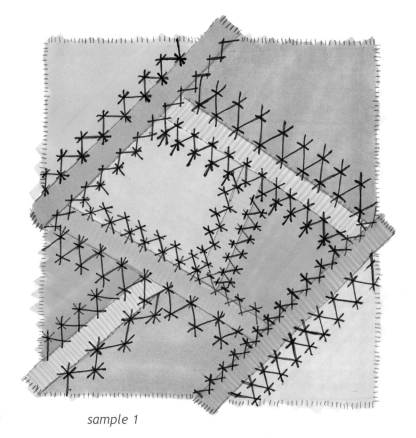

sample 1

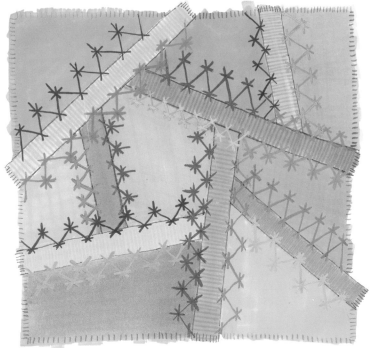

sample 2

All-ribbon-fabric crazy patchwork

You will need three separate lengths of premade ribbon fabric (see page 15). The ribbon fabric is made from a range of Jacquard, grosgrain, and tartan ribbons in three sets of colors: reds, blues, and greens. To make the very busy design look more cohesive, the same Jacquard ribbons have been used in each of the three different colorways, and the two outer edges of each ribbon-fabric length are made with grosgrain ribbon so the patch edges are always a solid color.

Use the woven edge of each ribbon-fabric patch to overlap the raw edges of the adjacent one, and angle the direction of the striped ribbons to give the design an overall liveliness, with no vertical direction.

SIZE
12-in (30-cm) square

METHOD
Machine stitching

MATERIALS
▶ Three strips of ribbon fabric (see page 15) in three color-ways, each measuring approx. 18 x 5½in (45 x 13.5cm), with outer edges of each piece made with a plain grosgrain ribbon
▶ 13-in (33-cm) square of fusible fabric
▶ Additional 6-in (15-cm) lengths of each color of grosgrain ribbon
▶ Machine sewing threads: matching cotton thread and monofilament (see page 12)

How to make

1 Cut through each of the ribbon fabrics at random angles to make a few patches; extra cuttings can be made as the work progresses [fig 1].

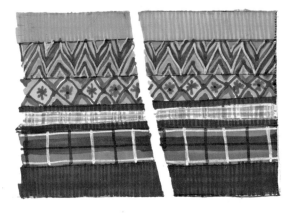

fig 1

2 Place the square of fusible fabric shiny-side up and position one of the ribbon-fabric patches at the edge of the square, making sure that the widest woven edge is toward the center of the square [fig 2].

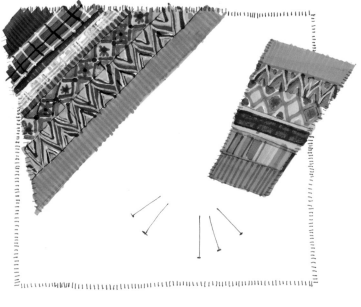

fig 2

3 Start to fill the square of backing fabric by positioning each random ribbon-fabric patch next to a different colorway, angling the stripes in adjacent patches in different directions [fig 3].

4 Continue in this way, pinning pieces into position as you work, until the backing fabric is covered. When complete, baste all the fabric pieces into position and remove the pins. Lightly press the surface before turning the piece over and pressing the backing fabric firmly to secure the pieces into position.

5 Using a matching cotton thread in the bobbin and a monofilament thread in the needle, machine-stitch the woven ribbon edges of each patch using a small, narrow zigzag stitch [fig 4]. When complete, remove all basting stitches and steam press the work lightly on the back with a pressing cloth.

> TIP **Filling gaps**
> As you create the crazy patchwork, you may find you get a gap or two. You can fill these in using a piece of matching ribbon and patching it over the gap, taking care to turn over any raw edges to align with the adjacent patch.

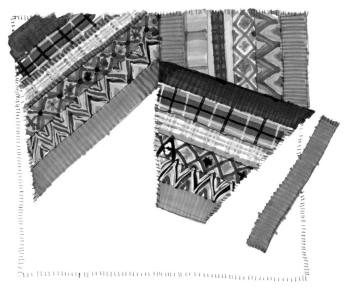

fig 3

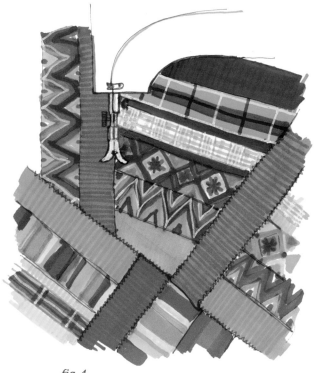

fig 4

Crazy patchwork fan with ribbons

This fan design and the one that follows are both based on the recurring fan motif of the original nineteenth-century crazy quilts. Japanese folding fans had been imported into the West at this time and were developed as a popular motif for crazy quilters. This simple version uses six different Jacquard ribbons, paired with five different solid fabrics, appliquéd to a contrasting backing fabric. The finished piece is ideal for making a cushion cover or appliquéing to a bag.

SIZE
12-in (30-cm) square

METHOD
Machine stitching

MATERIALS
► Six 9-in (23-cm) lengths of ⅞-in (2.2-cm) wide Jacquard ribbons in different designs
► Five 4 x 9in (10 x 23cm) solid-colored cotton fabric pieces to harmonize with ribbon choices
► 13-in (33-cm) square of solid-color backing fabric in a contrasting color
► 13-in (33-cm) square of fusible fabric
► Machine sewing threads: matching cotton thread and monofilament (see page 12)
► Water-soluble marker pen
► Whole fan template A (see page 124)
► Fan-section template B (see page 125)
► Two background-fabric templates: inner section C (see page 125) and outer section D (see page124)

How to make

1 Trace and cut paper patterns of templates A and B. Mark all seam allowances and divisions of the wedge shapes onto the paper templates.

2 Place the square of fusible fabric shiny-side up. Transfer template A to the fusible fabric using a water-soluble marker pen, marking in the individual fan sections [fig 1] and aligning the straight edges.

3 Place template B on one of the solid-colored fabrics. Draw around it and cut out the shape. Repeat for the other four pieces of fabric.

4 Lay the five fabric fan sections on the fusible fabric so that the contrasting colors are just touching each other, with raw edges aligned. Pin in place, then press into position.

5 Arrange the Jacquard ribbons to cover the raw edges between the fan sections, and so they are just touching the inner semicircle at the base of the fan [fig 2].

6 Machine stitch along the very edge of the ribbons, using mono-filament and very small straight stitches [fig 3].

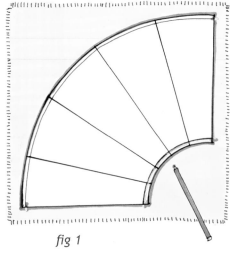

fig 1

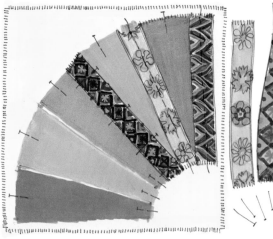

fig 2

fig 3

7 Trace and cut paper patterns of templates C and D (see page 124), with all seam allowances carefully marked. Pin onto the backing fabric and cut out each piece [fig 4].

8 Place both backing fabric pieces in position on top of the fan and the fusible fabric, and pin and baste in place. Using a very close machine zigzag gauge, top-stitch the two fabric pieces onto the ribbon appliqué [fig 5].

9 When complete, remove the basting stitches and steam press firmly on the back of the piece with a pressing cloth.

TIP **Neater finish**
This fan design, while appearing similar to the one that follows on pages 68-71 has a different design construction. The reason for this is that if you appliqué the top fabric to the fan patchwork, rather than vice versa, using a close zigzag stitch, you will achieve a much neater finish.

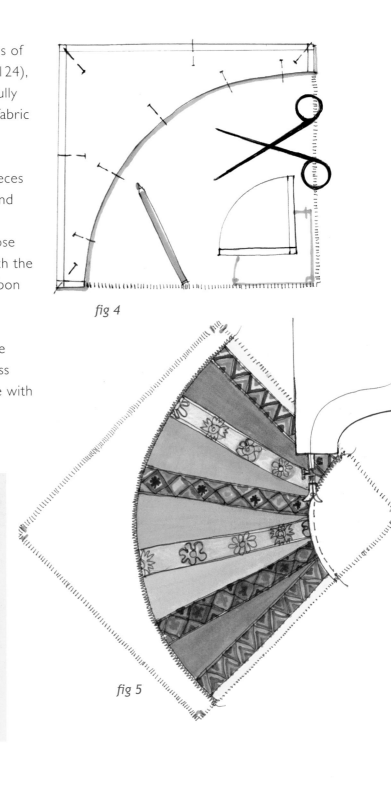

fig 4

fig 5

Embroidered crazy ribbon-fabric fan

This fan design is similar to the previous piece, but this time some of the fan sections are made from ribbon fabric (see page 15) in two colorways, using a range of Jacquard, grosgrain, and tartan ribbons. The narrower tartan ribbons have been appliquéd onto wider, plain grosgrain ribbons. As with the previous fan, harmonizing solid-colored cotton fabrics have been used in between the ribbons. This fan is also decorated with different herringbone stitches (see page 17), worked in various colored threads to harmonize with the design.

SIZE
12-in (30-cm) square

METHOD
Hand stitching

MATERIALS
▶ Two 7 x 9-in (18 x 23-cm) lengths of ribbon fabric in different colorways, made from Jacquard, striped, plain grosgrain, and tartan ribbons
▶ Three 4 x 9-in (10 x 23-cm) fabric pieces in different solid colors to harmonize with the ribbons
▶ 13-in (33-cm) square of backing fabric, to contrast with the ribbon fabrics and solid-colored fabrics
▶ 13-in (33-cm) square of fusible fabric
▶ Stranded embroidery floss in matching colors
▶ Water-soluble marker pen
▶ Whole fan template A (see page 126)
▶ Fan-section templates B and C (see page 126)

How to make

1 Trace and cut out all templates on page 126. Mark all seam allowances and divisions of the wedge shapes onto the paper templates [fig 1].

2 Place the square of fusible fabric shiny-side up. Transfer template A to the fusible fabric using a water-soluble pen or pencil, taking care to mark in the individual fan sections, but omitting the seam allowances and aligning the straight edges.

3 Place template B on top of the first piece of ribbon fabric, draw around it then flip it top to tail and draw a second shape; cut out. Repeat on the second ribbon fabric to give you four pieces, with alternating designs [fig 2].

4 Place template C on the three solid-colored fabrics in turn; draw around and cut out each individual wedge shape [fig 3]. Using the picture on page 69 as a guide, arrange the ribbon-fabric wedges on top of the fusible fabric on the marked fan shape. Pin and press lightly into position.

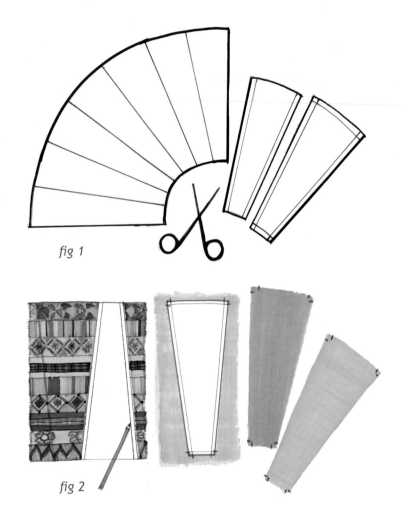

fig 1

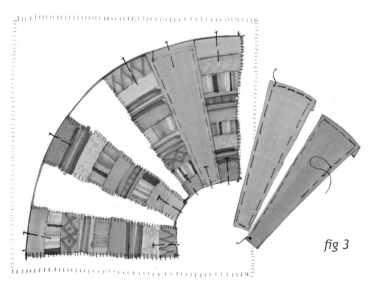

fig 2

fig 3

5 Now turn under and press small ¼-in (6-mm) seams on each edge of the three solid-colored fabric wedges and place them between the ribbon-fabric wedges, with their folded edges overlapping the raw edges of the ribbon fabric. Check that all are turned in before pinning and basting in position. Embroider between the separate wedge shapes using herringbone stitch variations (see page 17) in the various harmonizing colors [fig 4].

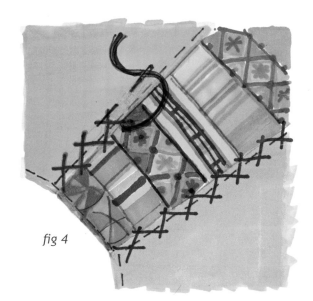

fig 4

6 Cut around the fan shape, removing all excess fusible fabric, and position the whole embroidered fan on the backing fabric. Making sure all turnings are neat, pin and baste; then embroider the edges using a tied herringbone stitch (see page 17) in one color to secure in position [fig 5]. Press on the wrong side when complete.

fig 5

TIP **Alternative design**
You could swap the ribbon fabrics in this fan for other contrasting colorways of plain fabric and work the herringbone stitches in one color only, as shown in the Hand-embroidered Crazy Patchwork sample shown on page 59.

Square ribbon patchworks

This section features various forms of ribbon squares. This small woven ribbon square is a really good way to try out simple combinations of ribbon types and colors. You could make it up in several different color schemes and then mount them as pictures (see pages 110-111), displayed in a group.

There are just two ribbons and one piece of fabric, so after you have chosen the woven Jacquard ribbon you just need to find two other colors that work with it, one for the grosgrain ribbon and another for the fabric background.

SIZE
7-in (18-cm) square

METHOD
Machine stitching and weaving

MATERIALS
▶ Two 7-in (18-cm) pieces of ⅞-in (2.2-cm) wide flowered Jacquard ribbon

▶ Four 7-in (18-cm) pieces of 1-in (2.5-cm) wide grosgrain ribbon, in a color to match one of the Jacquard ribbon flowers

▶ 7-in (18-cm) square of solid-colored fabric (choose one of the Jacquard ribbon pattern colors)

▶ 7-in (18-cm) square of fusible fabric (optional)

▶ Machine sewing threads: matching cotton thread and monofilament (see page 12)

How to make

1 Fold the fabric square in half vertically and crease with your finger. Repeat horizontally to find the center of the square. Place one Jacquard flower ribbon vertically down the center. Place the second Jacquard ribbon horizontally across the center crease [fig 1], over the first ribbon, and pin both ribbons in place at each end.

2 Place two grosgrain ribbons on either side of the vertical Jacquard ribbon. Weave the other two grosgrain ribbons horizontally, under the vertical Jacquard ribbon, on either side of the horizontal Jacquard ribbon. Pin and baste at each end [fig 2].

3 Machine-stitch over all the ribbon edges using a small zigzag stitch to catch each ribbon edge, in either monofilament or matching cotton threads [fig 3].

4 Lightly press the back of the square. To give the fabric more stability, if required, press a square of fusible fabric to the back of the piece when complete.

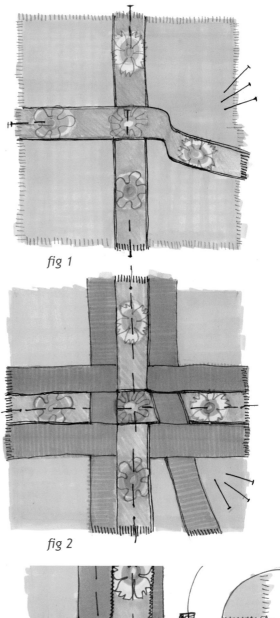

fig 1

fig 2

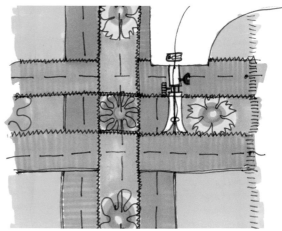

fig 3

Woven ribbon square

As with all the design samples in this book, we started by picking out a Jacquard ribbon that we liked. The choice of color for the grosgrain ribbons was determined by our choice of colors for the patterned ones to make sure it complemented them. Decoration has been added in the form of shisha mirrors in a grid-like pattern to give the design emphasis, but you could use buttons instead if you prefer. The resulting textured and colorful fabric would make a great picture to frame (see pages 110-111) or the basis of a cushion or appliqué design.

SIZE
Approx. 9½-in (24-cm) square

METHOD
Machine stitching, weaving, and hand stitching

MATERIALS
▶ Four 10-in (25-cm) lengths of ⅞-in (2.2-cm) wide striped ribbon
▶ Two 10-in (25-cm) lengths of 1½-in (4-cm) wide grosgrain ribbon in two contrasting solid colors to match the striped ribbon
▶ Two 10-in (25-cm) lengths of 1-in (2.5-cm) wide grosgrain ribbon in two contrasting colors to match the striped ribbon
▶ Two 10-in (25-cm) lengths of 1-in (2.5-cm) wide checked ribbon to contrast with the striped ribbon
▶ One 10-in (25-cm) length of 1-in (2.5-cm) wide grosgrain ribbon to match the two checked colors
▶ 10-in (25-cm) square of fusible fabric
▶ Machine sewing threads: cotton thread and monofilament
▶ Nine shisha mirrors or buttons to match the ribbons

How to make

1 Fold the fusible fabric square in half vertically and press the fold with your finger to crease it. Repeat horizontally. Place one piece of 1½-in (4-cm) wide grosgrain ribbon vertically down the center of the square, and pin. Place the second contrasting 1½-in (4-cm) wide grosgrain ribbon on the horizontal crease, over the first piece. Pin [fig 1].

2 Place the striped ribbons on either side (vertically and horizontally) of the solid-colored central ribbons, weaving them in and out of each other as shown. Pin into position before adding the next row of 1-in (2.5-cm) wide solid-colored grosgrain ribbons. Continue to add the ribbons, working outward from the center, weaving them in and out as you go [fig 2] and basting each section in place as you complete it.

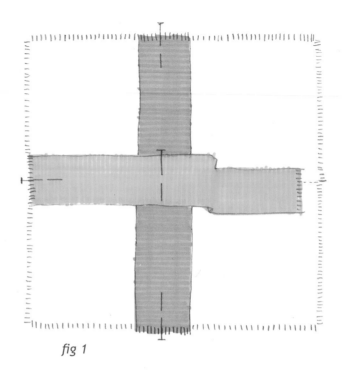

fig 1

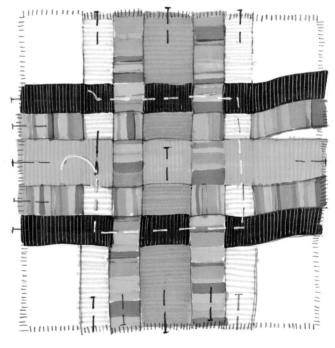

fig 2

3 Continue until all ribbons are woven in and secured [fig 3]. Then turn the fabric over and press lightly. Remove all pins and basting threads. Turn to the right side.

4 Pin the shisha mirrors on the ribbons (see the photograph on page 75 for placement) and stitch into position through the ribbons and the backing material [fig 4].

fig 4

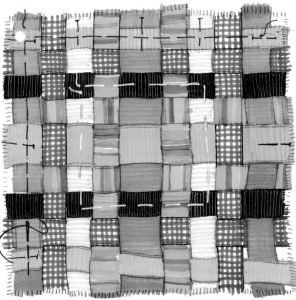

fig 3

ALTERNATIVE DECORATIONS

You can find other forms of decoration for this design. As well as buttons in harmonizing or contrasting colors, small ties made from leftover narrow tartan ribbons would look good. Choose a contrasting color for the decorations to the squares on which you propose to place them. You can add create repeating patterns with the additional decorations to emphasize the squares within the overall design.

Log cabin squares

This design consists of four blocks of ribbon-fabric squares, all constructed in the same way, and joined to make a pieced block. These four squares can be set together in whatever pattern you choose and joined using sashing strips of matching plain grosgrain ribbon, machine-stitched with a fine zigzag stitch. We mounted color variations of the single square as pictures (see pages 110-111) and turned the larger four-square block into a cushion cover (see page 98).

SIZE
Four 6½-in (16.5-cm) squares pieced with ribbon to make one large 13½-in (34.5-cm) square

METHOD
Machine stitching

MATERIALS
For each of the four squares

▶ Strip of ribbon fabric (see page 15) measuring 20 x 2¾in (51 x 7cm), made from two harmonizing ⅞-in (2.2-cm) wide Jacquard ribbons and one 1-in (2.5-cm) wide grosgrain ribbon with an appliqué of a narrow tartan ribbon (see page 27)

▶ 1½-in (4-cm) long piece of 1-in (2.5-cm) wide grosgrain ribbon, to blend with Jacquard ribbon colors

▶ 6-in (15-cm) square of fusible fabric

▶ Machine sewing threads: matching cotton thread and monofilament (see page 12)

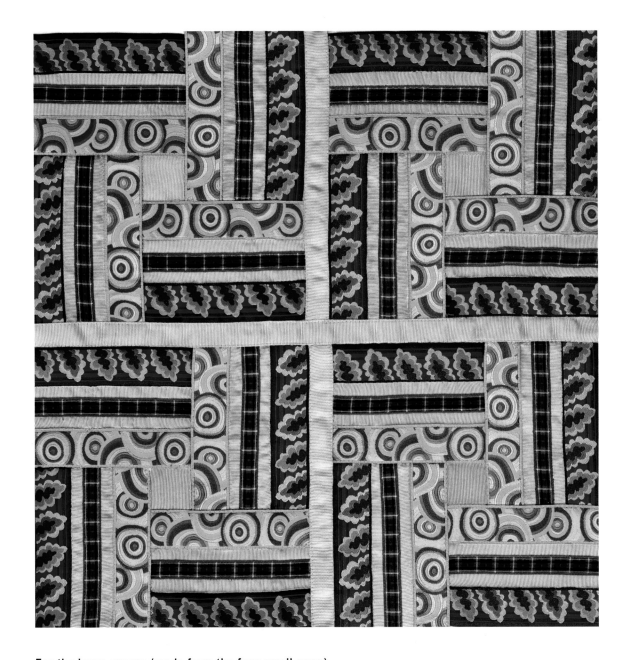

For the large square (made from the four small ones)

▶ Four 6½-in (16.5-cm) log cabin squares (see opposite)

▶ 30-in (76-cm) length of 1½-in (4-cm) wide grosgrain ribbon (color to match the center square of the four small squares)

▶ Machine sewing threads: matching cotton thread and monofilament

How to make

Piecing for each log cabin square (make 4)

1 Cut the length of ribbon fabric into four equal 5-in (12.5-cm) lengths [fig 1].

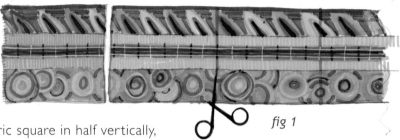

fig 1

2 Fold the fusible fabric square in half vertically, fingerpress to crease it, and repeat horizontally to find the center. Place the small rectangle of grosgrain ribbon in the center and pin in place. Arrange a length of ribbon fabric along one long side of the grosgrain rectangle [fig 2]; pin in place.

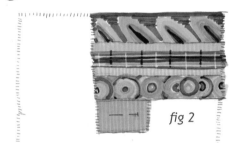

fig 2

3 Take the second piece of ribbon fabric, turn it so that the ribbon runs in a different direction, and place it so that it covers the raw edge of the grosgrain rectangle, as well as the edges of the first strip [fig 3]. Pin in place.

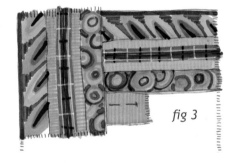

fig 3

4 Pin the remaining ribbon-fabric strips around the central piece of ribbon, turning each time, and making sure that all raw edges are covered by the ribbon edge of the next strip. Baste everything into position, remove pins, turn the piece over, and press lightly to hold the ribbons in place.

5 Machine-stitch the edges of the ribbons using a straight stitch, starting at the central square of grosgrain ribbon [fig 4], and either using matching cotton or monofilament thread. Remove all basting threads. Repeat Steps 1–5 to make three more squares.

fig 4

Piecing the large square

6 Place two log-cabin squares together, right side up, and pin an 8-in (20-cm) length of grosgrain ribbon over the edges of the join, measuring carefully. Pin, baste, and machine-stitch the ribbon to both squares using a narrow zigzag stitch along the edge. Repeat with the other two squares [fig 5].

7 Place the two sets of log cabin squares together and pin the remaining length of grosgrain ribbon over the join, then baste and machine stitch as before [fig 6].

fig 5

TIP Alternative design
The choice of color for the ribbon sashing will have an important effect on the whole design. A lighter colored ribbon will help to make the design more vibrant while a darker one will make it more somber. You can use this choice to play colors up or down accordingly.

fig 6

Ribbon star in a square

This six-pointed star is taken directly from a traditional patch-work block. You could use it as such, or do what we did and turn it into a very effective circular cushion (see page 101). The contrasting grosgrain ribbons match two colors in the striped ribbon—so choose the striped or patterned ribbon first. Place a contrasting checked or tartan ribbon between them for a zingy effect. This star is made from one length of ribbon fabric, which is then cut into diamonds and appliquéd onto a solid-colored fabric background. You may need to back it with fusible fabric (see page 12) if the fabric is lightweight.

SIZE
16in (40cm) at widest point

METHOD
Machine stitching

MATERIALS
► Strip of ribbon fabric measuring 32 x 4in (81 x 10cm),
made from:
   Inner strip: one 32-in (81-cm) length of multi-striped ribbon,
     ⅞in (2.2cm) wide
   Middle strips: two 32-in (81-cm) lengths of contrasting checked ribbon,
     ½in (1.2cm) wide
   Outer strips: two 32-in (81-cm) lengths of two different colors of
     ½-in (1.2-cm) wide grosgrain ribbon, to harmonize with the striped ribbon
► 18-in (45.5-cm) square of backing fabric
► 4-in (10-cm) square of fusible fabric
► Machine sewing threads: matching cotton thread and monofilament
(see page 12)
► Water-soluble marker pen
► Diamond template A (see page 127)

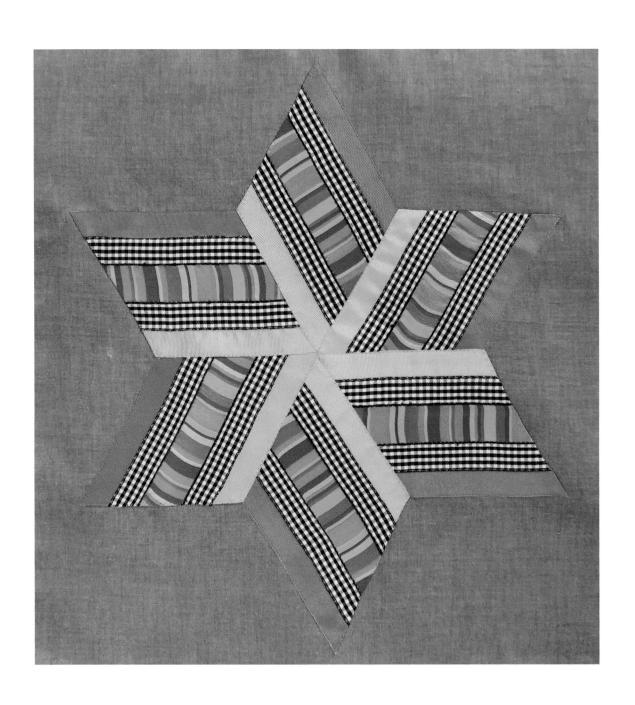

How to make

1 Copy the diamond template onto a piece of card and mark six diamonds on the ribbon fabric strip, as shown, and cut out [fig 1].

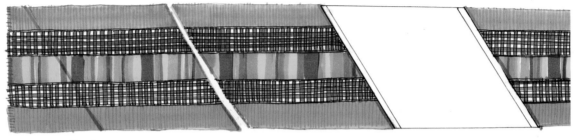

fig 1

Preparing the star tips

2 Fold over a ¼-in (6-mm) seam allowance on one raw edge of each diamond, then press and baste in place [fig 2].

3 Cut a small piece of fusible fabric and place it over the back of the narrow point of each star prepared in Step 2, and press firmly.

4 Trim away all excess fabric so that the narrow point of each diamond appears neat from the front [fig 3].

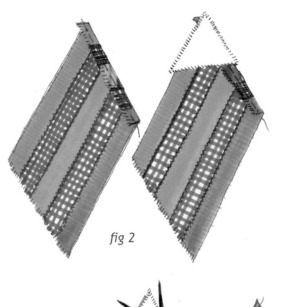

fig 2

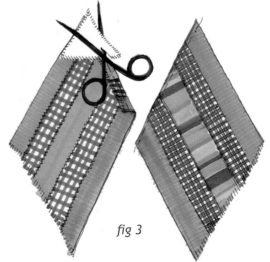

fig 3

Assembling the star

5 Fold the fabric background square in half vertically, crease the fold, and then repeat horizontally. Mark each crease with a water-soluble marker pen. Position the first diamond so that the prepared point will form one outer tip of the star, pin, and baste [fig 4]. Continue to arrange the other diamonds to complete the star, ensuring the second overlaps the raw edge of the first and so on around the shape.

6 Machine stitch along the inner edges of the grosgrain ribbons [fig 5], using a matching thread or monofilament and a small straight stitch on the edge of the fabric.

7 Work the rest of the appliqué by straight stitching over the outer edges of the grosgrain ribbons, and then use a small zigzag stitch over the folded edges [fig 6] so that everything is secure.

8 Remove all basting stitches and press lightly on the back of the fabric.

TIP **Alternative design**

If you want to develop this design for another set of ribbons, make sure the inner and outer edges of each star segment are in solid colors. This helps to hold the star shape and gives the design vibrancy at the same time.

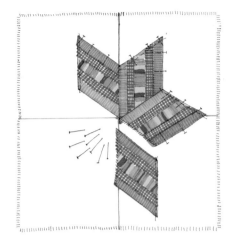

fig 4

fig 5

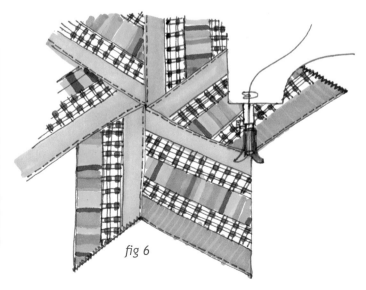

fig 6

Windmill square

This design is based on a traditional windmill patchwork pattern, with ribbon fabrics alternating with solid-colored cotton fabrics that harmonize with the ribbon-fabric colors. This makes a very strong directional design, particularly in contrasting colors. A more muted version could be created using different shades of a single color.

If the solid-colored cotton is much thinner than the ribbon fabric, it will need to be reinforced by pressing squares of fusible fabric to the back of each piece before you begin.

This patchwork block looks great as a cushion (see page 96) but could be appliquéd to an apron or bag just as well.

SIZE
12¼-in (31-cm) square (completed design)

METHOD
Machine stitching

MATERIALS
▶ Strip of ribbon fabric (see page 15) measuring 14 x 6¼in (35.5 x 16cm) made from patterned and plain Jacquard and grosgrain ribbons of different widths, chosen to harmonize); start and finish the ribbon fabric with grosgrain ribbons
▶ Four 8-in (20-cm) squares of solid-colored cotton fabrics in colors to harmonize with the ribbons
▶ Approx. ¼yd (25cm) fusible fabric (optional)
▶ Machine sewing threads: matching cotton thread and monofilament (see page 12)
▶ Water-soluble marker pen
▶ Triangle template A (see page 127)

How to make

1 Cut out the template and position on the ribbon fabric as shown, with the inner line aligned with the lower edge. With a water-soluble pen, mark a triangle and then flip the template to mark the second triangle, top to tail [fig 1]. Repeat to make four triangles. Cut out.

2 Use the whole template to cut out triangles from the four solid-colored cotton fabrics [fig 1].

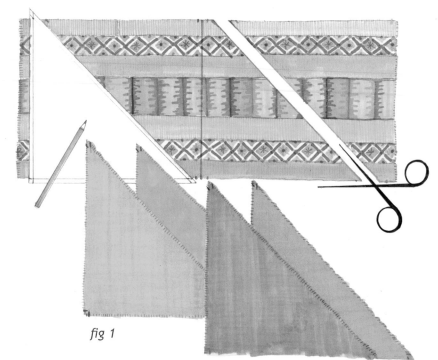

fig 1

3 With long sides together [fig 2], position a fabric triangle right-side up and a matching ribbon triangle right side down on top of it. Stitch along the longest side using a straight stitch and a ¼-in (6-mm) seam allowance [fig 3]. Open out to create a square. Repeat to create all four squares. Press the seams open at the back.

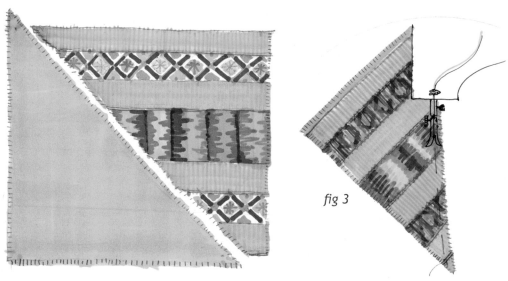

fig 2

fig 3

4 Arrange the squares to form the larger square (shown on page 87). Stitch the squares together in pairs using a ¼-in (6-mm) seam allowance, and press the seams open. Then place the pieces right sides together, and align the central points very carefully, basting into position if necessary. Stitch together as before [fig 4]. Open out and press the seam open.

5 Turn and press the back of the square, snipping the seam allowance at the center so that the seam allowances can be pressed to either side to lie flat [fig 5].

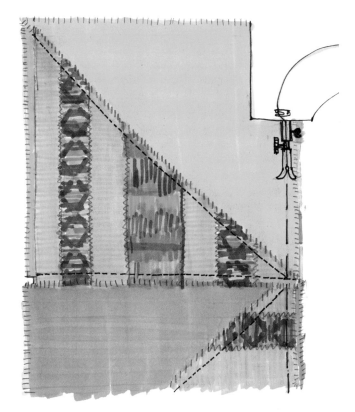

fig 4

TIP Alternative block layout
As this design is composed of four squares, you can put these together in different ways to vary the composition in much the same way that traditional patchwork blocks are used on quilts. For a bigger version of this design, you could turn the squares so that the solid-colored segments create strong diagonal stripes, for example.

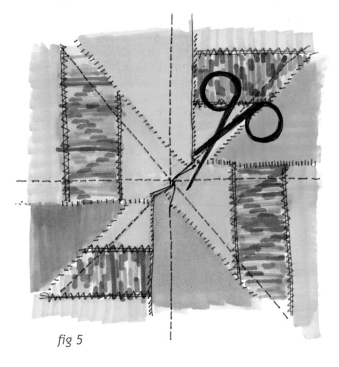

fig 5

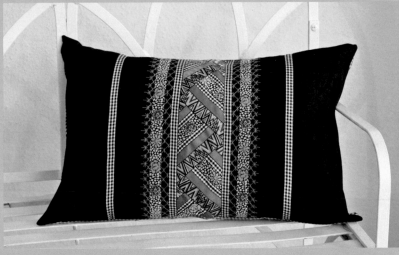

creating appliqués and projects

In this section, many of the ribbon fabrics made in the first section have been translated into projects for you or your home, either applied to bought items such as cushion covers, lamp-shades, or bags, or used to create stand-alone items like hat bands or mounted pictures. The techniques for creating appliqués with ribbon fabrics are also included here.

Appliqué techniques

The following pages explain how to create appliqué shapes and show the different methods of applying the appliqués to a base fabric. You will find the templates on pages 124-127. Use a water-soluble pen to transfer any marks onto your fabric.

CREATING AN APPLIQUÉ

If the appliqué is needed at the center of a garment or cushion, then you will need to find and mark the exact center of both the base fabric and the appliquéd shape (see page 40). This method does not require seam allowances.

1 Draw around the template to transfer the appliqué shape onto the paper backing of a piece of fusible web [fig 1].
2 Press the back of the piece of fusible web to bond it to the wrong side of the appliqué or ribbon fabric. Cut out the fabric shape [fig 2].
3 Remove the paper backing from the cut shape, then position it on the base fabric, aligning with any markings. Lightly pin, or for intricate shapes, baste in place [fig 3], before pressing.
4 For a stronger and more defined finish, machine stitch with a close zigzag stitch [fig 4], or hand-stitch or embroider around the edge of the shape.

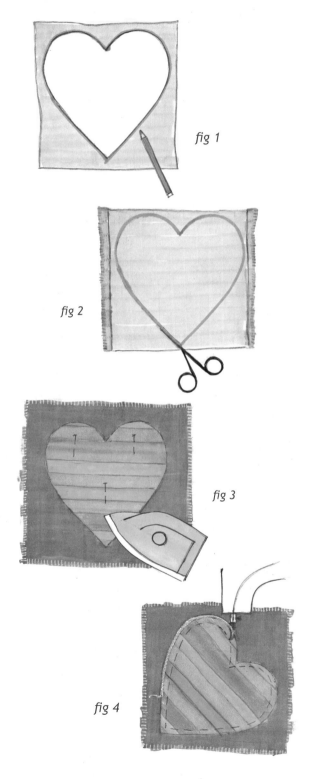

fig 1

fig 2

fig 3

fig 4

MAKING AN APPLIQUÉ POCKET

If you are using one of the square ribbon-fabric designs or a plain fabric to make a pocket, you can fold over a seam allowance all around (or attach a border as shown on pages 94-95) and attach a piece of ribbon to the top edge to form a facing. You will need to calculate the amount of facing ribbon by measuring the ribbon fabric and adding seam allowances.

1 Take a square of ribbon fabric and press a piece of fusible fabric of the same size onto the back.

2 Cut a piece of 1-in (2.5-cm) wide lightweight ribbon to the width of the pocket top (plus ¼ in/6mm allowance at each end). Top-stitch the lower edge of the ribbon to the right side of the top edge of the fabric [fig 1].

3 Turn the ribbon to the wrong side and press. Then either machine stitch or hand stitch into position [fig 2].

4 Turn under a ½-in (1.2-cm) wide hem all around the other three pocket edges. Find the center of the base fabric and the center of the sample (see page 40). Pin together at the top edge and through the center, then pin and baste all the edges into position [fig 3].

5 Machine stitch around three sides, starting and finishing at the pocket top with a reverse stitch. Stitch a second row of top-stitches within the first row by placing the outer edge of the machine foot on the first line of stitching [fig 4]. Press.

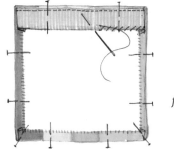

fig 1

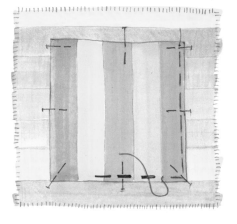

fig 2

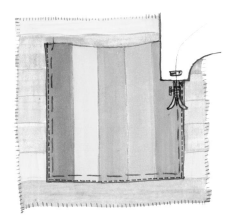

fig 3

fig 4

ADDING RIBBON BORDERS

Some of the cushion projects are created using a ribbon-fabric sample, which is then finished with a ribbon border. Here, we show two different types of border. It may be necessary to strengthen some ribbon fabrics by applying a matching size piece of fusible backing to the wrong side before adding the borders.

fig 1

Ribbon border 1

This border is created for a fabric square from four lengths of ribbon, each cut to the length of the edges of the finished sample plus the width of the ribbon used and seam allowances.

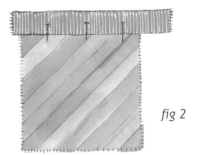

fig 2

1 Place the sample on a flat surface, measure, and cut four equal lengths of ribbon.

2 Position the first border ribbon by abutting it to the edge of the sample [fig 1] but with a ¼-in (6-mm) seam allowance protruding beyond the left-hand corner [fig 2] to cover any raw edges.

3 Machine stitch the ribbon into position, using a small zigzag stitch in either a matching thread or monofilament [fig 3]. Press lightly with a damp cloth.

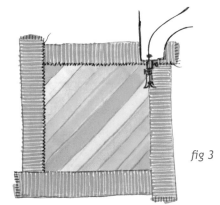

fig 3

4 Place the sample onto the prepared base fabric. Pin and baste it into position, turning the ends of the ribbons neatly to the back of the border. Machine stitch the border onto the base fabric on the outside edges using a straight stitch [fig 4].

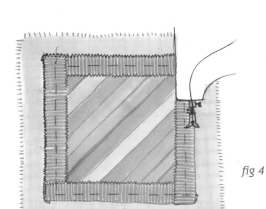

fig 4

Ribbon border 2

This border is also used for a square patchwork. Cut the border ribbon into two pieces equal to the length of one side of the sample (plus ¼-in/6-mm seam allowances), and two other pieces equal to the length of the side plus twice the width of the ribbon used, plus seam allowances [fig 1].

fig 1

1 Position the shorter border ribbons by abutting them to the top and bottom edges of the square [fig 2] with the seam allowance protruding at each end. Machine stitch the inner edges to the fabric square.

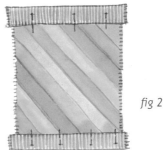

fig 2

2 Repeat to attach the two longer borders to the remaining edges [fig 3].

3 Machine stitch the border onto the base fabric [fig 4].

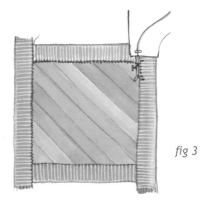

fig 3

For a pocket border

The pocket border is made in a similar way to the Ribbon border 2, except that you work on only the pocket sides and base.

1 Cut lengths of ribbon following the instructions for Ribbon border 2, above. Pin one length to the lower edge of the pocket fabric and the background fabric and baste into position.

2 Pin the remaining ribbon lengths on either side of the pocket, and machine stitch the inner edges to the ribbon fabric sample.

3 Turn hems on the raw edges of the ribbons and press.

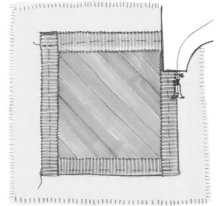

fig 4

Cushions

We have used the ribbon-fabric samples to make several cushion shapes. Your fabric samples can be either appliquéd to a store-bought cushion cover of a suitable color and size, or you can make up your own cushion front with an envelope back for a tailormade version (see page 128). We have included some specially shaped cushions, which are better stuffed. You can cut up a ribbon-fabric sample to make the heart-shaped cushion on pages 100-103) or, for a round cushion, appliqué the sample to a backing fabric. Several of the cushions have borders added to give them a finishing touch (see pages 94-95). For cushions other than the stuffed ones, you will need to purchase a cushion form of the appropriate size.

APPLIQUÉ SQUARE CUSHIONS

These cushions are made from the ribbon-fabric designs shown in the first chapter, with or without added borders. You can make up an envelope back (see page 128) if you are using the ribbon-fabric design as the cushion front.

Windmill cushion

This square cushion is made from the design sample on pages 86-89. A border has been added using the striped Jacquard ribbon, so that the cushion measures 15in (38cm) square. You will need a 58-in (148-cm) length of the 1½-in (4-cm) wide striped Jacquard ribbon. Follow the method for cutting and making the Ribbon border 1 on page 94.

Windmill cushion

OPPOSITE This cushion is bordered with the striped ribbon used in the design sample on pages 86-89.

Log cabin cushion

ABOVE This cushion is bordered with matching wider ribbon used in the four-square design sample on pages 78-81.

Crazy ribbon-fabric patchwork fan cushion

ABOVE This version of the crazy fan design sample has been made

into a neat, small cushion. Its sister design is shown on page 91.

Log cabin cushion

This cushion is made from the four-block design sample on pages 78-81. It has a border made from 1-in (2.5-cm) wide grosgrain ribbon in the same color as the narrow ribbon used to sash the individual log cabin blocks. With the border, the cushion cover measures 16in (40cm) square. You will need a 64-in (163-cm) length of the 1-in (2.5-cm) wide grosgrain ribbon in pale blue for the border. Apply it following the method for Ribbon border 1 on page 94.

Crazy fan cushion

The two crazy patchwork fan design samples on pages 64-71 have each been converted into cushions. Each completed block includes a front fabric backing with a seam allowance of ½in (1.2cm) included in the sample instructions, so you can add your own envelope cushion back (see page 128) in matching fabric. The cushions measure 12in (30cm) square.

CUSHIONS FROM EXTENDED SAMPLES

For the following cushions, the ribbon-fabric pieces have been adapted slightly so that they fit a regular rectangular cushion form.

Diagonal ribbon strip cushion

This large rectangular cushion is made using the design sample on pages 32-35, extended to fit a regular-sized long cushion form measuring 26 × 14in (60 × 40cm) by adding two strips of background fabric, joined to the patchwork with a 16-in (40-cm) strip of ½-in (1.2-cm) wide checked ribbon appliquéd over each join. You will need ¼yd (25cm) of extra background fabric to extend the cushion front.

Trim the background fabric on the patchwork to measure 13in (33cm). Cut two pieces of extra background fabric to measure 6 × 16in (15 × 40cm) and stitch to the main fabric on each side. Then apply the ribbon over each join. Make an envelope cushion back (see page 128).

Diagonal ribbon strip cushion

LEFT This large cushion uses the design sample on pages 32-35 as a central strip, with extra border fabric at the sides with further checked ribbons appliquéd over the joins.

Flying geese cushion

This is made from the design sample on pages 28-31. We added a narrow strip of ribbon fabric made from two ribbons (one Jacquard and one grosgrain ribbon) to the top and bottom of the patchwork, so that the finished piece measures 18 x 12in (46 x 30cm).

For the additional ribbon fabric strips, you will need ½yd (½m) of $^7/_8$-in (2.2-cm) wide Jacquard ribbon to match one of the ribbons in the patchwork, plus ½yd (½m) of ½-in (1.2-cm) wide solid-colored grosgrain ribbon, and ½yd (½m) each of two solid-colored fabrics from the patchwork (for the envelope cushion back). Apply the extra strips of ribbon fabric so that the plain ribbon is next to the patterned area.

STUFFED CUSHIONS

These cushions do not have removable covers. The heart and the buttoned circular cushions can more easily be made this way, although you could buy cushion forms in a variety of shapes and make your own removable cover by following the instructions for the envelope cushion covers (see page 128) using the cushion form shape as a template (plus seam allowances).

Crazy heart cushion

This cushion is made from the design sample on pages 56-9, cut into the shape of a heart and stuffed. It does not have a removable cover. The size is approximately 12 x 12in (30 x 30cm). You will need the large heart

template (page 125) plus a piece of backing fabric 13in (33cm) square, and stuffing. Follow the instructions on page 102 for making up.

Large ribbon yo-yo cushion

This cushion uses the large yo-yo design sample on pages 42-45 to create a stuffed buttoned cushion with a diameter of 13in (33cm). You will need an extra ½yd (½m) of fabric for the cushion back, a large colored button, a darning or mattress needle, strong thread, a large sheet of paper for a template, and a circular cushion form (approximately 14in/35cm diameter).

To make the backing template, trace around the yo-yo onto a sheet of paper, add

a further 1in (2.5cm) for a small border plus a ½in (1.2cm) seam allowance to the outside edge, and cut out. Then follow the instructions for making a stuffed cushion on page102.

When complete, thread the long needle with strong thread, knot the end, and pass the needle through the center of the cushion from front to back. Take a small stitch and bring the needle out at the front again, pulling the thread tightly. Sew on the button, passing the needle through the cushion and out to the front again to finish (see Sewing buttons, page 16).

Star cushion

This is made from the star design sample on pages 82-5. It is cut into a circle, using a template to make a circular stuffed cushion measuring 14in (35cm) in diameter. You will need ½yd (½m) of backing fabric, a sheet of paper larger than the cushion stuffing material, or a circular cushion form 14in (35cm) in diameter.

Cut a paper template 14½in (36.5cm) in diameter. Find and mark the center by folding twice (see page 40). Center the template on the patchwork, pin and draw around it with a water-soluble pen. Cut out the circle and then cut out a circle of backing fabric to the same size. Follow the instructions (see page 102) for stuffed cushions. Finally, follow the instructions for buttoning the yo-yo cushion.

Flying geese cushion

OPPOSITE This cushion features the design sample from pages 28-31, extended with fabric and ribbon strips on top and bottom.

Star cushion

LEFT This little stuffed cushion has been made from the design sample on pages 82-85. It does not have a removable cover.

MAKING A STUFFED CUSHION

1 Make a paper template (see page 125 for the heart shape), adding ½-in (1.2-cm) seam allowance; for a circle add an extra 1in (2.5cm) to the dimensions of the ribbon fabric piece, to allow for a narrow border and seam allowance.

2 Pin the template to both the top and backing fabrics and draw around it with a water-soluble pen. Cut out, making sure to mark a 4-in (10-cm) gap for the opening that is large enough for your hand to be inserted [fig 1].

3 With wrong sides together, machine stitch around the shape, starting and finishing at the marks for the openings [fig 2].

4 Snip into the seam allowance, taking care not to cut the stitching—this enables the cushion to be turned out to a perfect shape [fig 3].

5 Pull the cushion right sides out and stuff with wadding (or a suitably sized cushion form for a circular cushion). Turn under the seam allowance at the opening before closing the gap with small oversewing stitches.

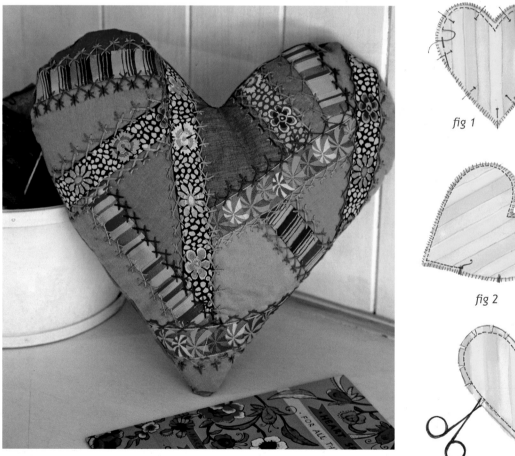

fig 1

fig 2

fig 3

Stuffed cushion

ABOVE This stuffed heart cushion has been created from the design sample on pages 56-59, cut to fit the shape.

Triple yo-yo cushion

OPPOSITE This cushion is made from the triple yo-yo design sample on pages 42-45.

Aprons

We have created a selection of aprons with either square pockets (large or small) or heart appliqués (large or small) made from the ribbon fabric. You can use either a purpose-made piece of ribbon fabric or a portion of one of the patchwork designs. The pockets on these aprons all use a color variation of the basic small square patchwork on pages 72-73. The hearts are cut from a piece of ribbon fabric and appliquéd in place on a store-bought apron. You can also add a ribbon trim to the apron hem, if you wish. Choose different ribbon widths and designs and the color of the background fabric to suit the color of your apron. For children's aprons (opposite, top) we have used colors for the small heart appliqués that contrast with the bright colors of the aprons—red on blue, or blue on pink—for maximum vibrancy.

Apron with heart appliqués

RIGHT AND OPPOSITE (TOP) These aprons, with their heart appliqués, were made using leftover ribbon fabric. The apron (right) uses the large heart template on page 125 and the children's aprons (opposite, top) use the smaller template on on the same page. The hearts are finished off with close zigzag machine stitching.

APRON HEART APPLIQUÉS

To makes these aprons, follow the appliqué instructions on page 94, using pieces of ribbon fabric of your choice. The small and large heart templates are given on page 125.

APRON SQUARE POCKET APPLIQUÉS

Follow the instructions on page 95 to create these apron pockets, using a piece of ribbon fabric of your choice (such as a color variation of the square patchwork on pages 72-73).

Aprons with pockets

LEFT These apron pockets are made using a color variation of the square patchwork block on pages 72-73. You will need to turn over a hem on all four sides of the pocket, handstitching the top hem first, before machine stitching the sides of the pocket to the apron.

Lampshades

We used store-bought paper-backed fabric lampshades and decorated them in different ways, one with a yo-yo design (see pages 36-37), another using the embroidered ribbon strips designs (see pages 20-23), and the other with a simple decoration of two ribbons joined with a decorative embroidery stitch. To position your appliqués on the lampshade, you will first need to measure and mark the lampshade with a water-soluble pen. The ideas that follow can be adjusted to any size of shade, and, of course, color combinations chosen to suit your decor.

Yo-yo Lampshade

RIGHT A selection of single yo-yos made from wide Jacquard ribbon (see pages 36-37) have been stitched to a store-bought drum lampshade in three alternating rows, using buttons to secure them in place.

YO-YO LAMPSHADE

The size of the lampshade will determine how many yo-yos you need to make, and the spacing between each one and the number of rows. The yo-yos are sewn onto the lampshade through the centrally placed button (see below). If you prefer, glue them into position and omit the buttons—the light will then shine through the small central gap in spots. The lampshade shown measures 12in (30cm) diameter and is 9in (23cm) deep.

For a shade this size, you need 18 single ribbon yo-yos (each yo-yo requires 7in/17.5cm of $^7/_8$-in/2.2-cm wide Jacquard ribbon—see page 37 for instructions). You also need 18 medium two-hole buttons in colors to blend with the ribbons, with matching thread. Measure the shade and mark out three evenly spaced rows, with 6 yo-yos to a row, evenly distributed around the shade. Mark the placement dots for each yo-yo on the outside of the lampshade using a fabric marking pencil. Then sew the yo-yos to the lampshade, following the instructions below.

EMBROIDERED RIBBON LAMPSHADE

This is a really simple and effective use of the beautiful Jacquard ribbons. Two rows of ribbons are placed close together at the base of the shade, with the space between them embroidered using a simple row of Cretan stitches (see page 108), that join the ribbons without stitching the shade. You could use herringbone stitches, too. The paper lampshade shown measures 12in (30cm) diameter and is 9in (23cm) deep. You need three pieces of

---

SEWING A YO-YO TO A LAMPSHADE

1 Using a needle and strong thread with a knot at the end, hold the first yo-yo in position over the marked dot and pierce a hole through the center of the yo-yo from the front, passing the needle to the back and out to the front again about ¼in (6mm) away. Sew the button in place.

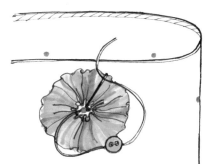

2 Pass the needle once more through the yo-yo center and the button, pull the thread to the front, knot it, and snip the ends. Repeat for each yo-yo.

woven Jacquard ribbon, each cut to the circumference of the shade plus a turning allowance of ½in (1.2cm) at the ends. You also need a skein of black embroidery floss, embroidery needle, a water-soluble pen, and some fabric glue.

Mark the position for the bottom ribbon with a line drawn using a water-soluble pen. Leave a gap of about ¾–1in (2–2.5cm) and then mark the position of each edge of the upper ribbon. Apply a narrow band of fabric glue to the lowest marked position of the bottom ribbon, taking care to keep the upper edge clear (for stitching). Working from the join in the shade, press the ribbon edge firmly against the lamp-shade all the way around, then fold over the raw end by ½in (1.2cm) and glue the ribbon join together on the lampshade seam. Repeat for the upper ribbon position (but leave the lower edge clear of glue). Glue a further length of ribbon to the top of the shade.

Take a length of embroidery floss and join the two lower ribbons using a Cretan stitch (see below), working the stitches between the two lower ribbons —the stitches are made through the two ribbons only; they are not worked through the shade.

Embroidered ribbon lampshade

LEFT The finished lampshade (above left) in which the lower ribbons are embroidered with Cretan stitch (left). The stitches are worked as shown, picking up a small piece of each of the two ribbons in turn.

Ribbon strips lampshade

OPPOSITE The design sample from pages 20-23 has been used for this shade, with the fabric extended at the sides.

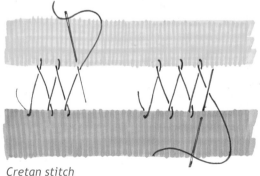

Cretan stitch

RIBBON STRIPS LAMPSHADE

This design has been adapted from the design sample on pages 20-23, to which extra background fabric is added to the sides to wrap around a lampshade. We chose the depth of shade to suit the sample but you could easily adapt the sample to suit the shade.

You will also need an extra length of one of the ribbons used, cut to the same length as the pieced ribbons, and two lengths of bias binding cut to the size of the shade's circumference plus a ¼-in (6-mm) seam allowance, plus a tube of quick-drying glue and some double-sided adhesive tape.

Measure the circumference of the shade, then adjust the extra fabric either side of the sample to fit it, adding the extra ribbon length to one end. Trim the width of the fabric to allow ½in (1.2cm) extra at the top and bottom edges. Machine stitch the two lengths of bias binding to the right side of the top and bottom edges, starting with the ribbon end. Trim away any surplus fabric and press.

Firmly press double-sided tape along the seam of the shade. Place the raw edge of the fabric on top of the tape and wrap around the shade. Secure with another strip of double-sided tape underneath the ribbon.

Put a line of fabric glue inside and underneath the metal wire inside the top of the shade. Turn the top of the fabric over the top lampshade edge and, using the bias binding, fold in and over the glued area. Make sure that all the bias binding is neatly tucked away under the metal wire. Repeat at the lower edge.

Mounted pictures

You can mount any of your samples in a simple frame, and put several pictures together for greater effect. The best frame to use for textiles is a box frame as it gives a space between the surface of the fabric and the glass, so the fabric does not appear crushed. The choice of mount card and size is an important factor in giving the sample extra impact. You can also vary the size and angle of the sample or cut it into smaller pieces and mount as a coordinated group.

MOUNTED SQUARES

The square ribbon design, two color variations of the log cabin design, and the woven square design (the latter cut down in size) were the inspiration for this set of four similarly mounted pictures.

Store-bought box frames usually come with their own window mounts. Follow the instructions opposite for how to mount a piece of patchwork in a regular square box frame.

Grouped pictures

RIGHT The pictures shown here are as follows: at top left and bottom right are variations of the log cabin design sample on pages 72-73, one of them angled, top right is the centre section of the woven design sample on pages 74-77 and at bottom left is the square ribbon patchwork design sample on pages 78-81.

Mounting a patchwork

1 Mark the backboard of the frame through the mount window with a water-soluble pen or pencil, taking care not to mark the mount [fig 1].

2 Using double-sided tape, make a cross within the marked square [fig 2] and mark each center edge of the board.

3 Cut a piece of padding or wadding 1in (2.5cm) smaller than the marked square [fig 3] and attach to the marked cross.

4 Attach strips of double-sided tape to the back of the patch-work fabric [fig 4]. Mark the center edges with a water-soluble pen.

5 Press the fabric firmly onto the backboard, aligning the center marks on the fabric with those on the backboard [fig 5].

6 Position the mount over the fabric and reassemble the frame in the box frame in the usual way [fig 6].

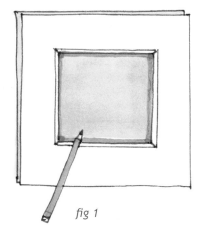

fig 1

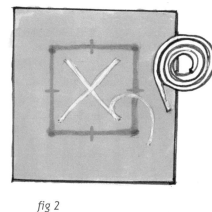

fig 2

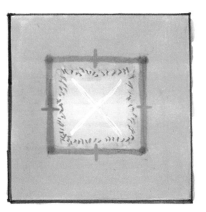

fig 3

fig 4

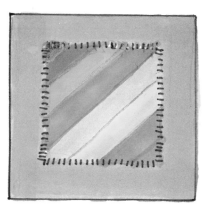

fig 5

fig 6

Bags

Plain store-bought fabric bags can be transformed with many of the patchwork designs from the first part of the book, either utilized as an outer pocket on the bag (by adding a ribbon border as a finishing) or appliquéd as a decorative patch or special shape—we, of course, used a decorative heart! The bags we used measure 16 x 14in (40 x 36cm), which is a useful size, and they are available in a range of colors: neutrals and brights. You can also embellish the bags with ribbons on the handles or as borders.

MOUNTED SQUARES

The large squares or pockets on the bags illustrated here have been made using several of the ribbon patchworks featured in the beginning of the book. Each patchwork fabric has been backed with a piece of fusible fabric, if it wasn't already included in the construction. This both strengthens and protects the pocket during regular use.

At Heart Space Studios we devised a system of adding ribbons to attach the design samples as pockets (see page 95).

Bag with bordered appliqué

Here we used the woven ribbon design sample on pages 74-77 and appliquéd it with a matching checked ribbon border. The bag was then embellished with more checked ribbons inside the handles (see page 114). Use a ribbon width that fits neatly inside the handle width. Checked and tartan ribbons are available in many different widths and colorways.

Bag with appliqué border

ABOVE The large woven square design sample (see pages 74-77) has been bordered with the checked ribbon to make an attractive front to a plain store-bought bag.

Bags with appliqué pockets

The blue bag has been embellished with a large pocket that uses the design sample from pages 24-27. The ribbon fabric has been turned into a pocket following the method for the ribbon bordered pocket described on page 95, using matching grosgrain and tartan ribbons.

For the pink bag, we attached the crazy ribbon sample design on pages 60-63 as a pocket, using extra tartan ribbons to attach it to the bag. We also machine stitched additional lengths of tartan ribbon to the inner bag handles and lined inside the top edge of the bag (see page 114) for a neat finish.

ADDING RIBBON EMBELLISHMENTS

These bags offer lots of opportunities for adding ribbon details. Choose harmonizing colors or match one of the ribbons from the main design.

Ribbon trim handles

When choosing ribbon, make sure that it is either the same width as the bag handles or slightly narrower.

Bags with appliqué pockets

ABOVE AND RIGHT For these two bags, the design samples on pages 24-70 and 60-63 have been turned into pockets on the front of the bag.

Measure the length of the handles and cut the ribbon to match plus extra for turnings. Pin and baste the ribbons into position on the handles, turning under a ½-in (1.2-cm) hem on the raw edges of the ends. (If adding a ribbon trim border, to the bag top, see below). Machine top-stitch each side of the ribbon using mono-filament in a straight stitch. Press.

Ribbon trim border

Carefully measure the circumference of the bag and cut a length of ribbon to match, plus seam allowance. Pin and baste the ribbon onto the outer edge of the bag, making sure that you trap the ribbon from the handles underneath, if you are trimming the handles (below). Machine stitch each side of the ribbon using monofila-ment in a straight stitch. Press.

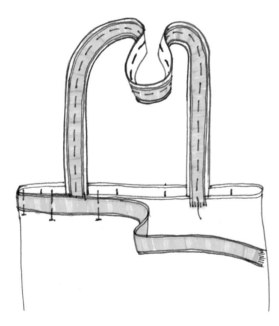

Pinning ribbon trim around top of bag

APPLIQUÉD SHAPES

You can add a specially shaped appliqué to a plain fabric bag for decoration from either the heart or fan templates used in this book.

Appliqué heart bag

For the bag opposite, use the large heart template on page 125. The piece of ribbon fabric for the heart has been made from the ribbon fabric on page 15, which has been cut in half and then stitched together to form a square from which the heart shape can be cut.

1 Take the length of ribbon fabric measuring 4½ x 18in (11.5 x 45cm) and fold in half length-wise. Cut across the fold, then machine appliqué the two pieces together so that you have a square measuring approximately 9 x 9in (23 x 23cm).

2 Trace the large heart template on page 125 and transfer to the fabric and fusible backing fabric (below).

3 Then follow the instructions on page 92 to cut out the heart from the square and appliqué it to the bag.

Tracing off templates

Appliqué heart bag

LEFT A simple heart ribbon-fabric appliqué on a plain bag, with the handles and top picked out in a matching Jacquard ribbon, adds an elegant touch to the design.

Espadrilles

The simplest and quickest ribbon fabric to make is a ribbon yo-yo (see page 37), which can be attached with a button to fabric espadrilles for an easy project that even children can enjoy. For more experienced stitchers, the embroidered versions look more sophisticated, but are still fresh and summery.

BUTTONED YO-YO

This simple design has one yo-yo attached to the upper with a button. You will need two single yo-yos made with 1½-in (4-cm) wide ribbon or two double yo-yos (see pages 36-37) to a similar size, and a button for each yo-yo, about ¾in (2cm) wide, in colors to match the ribbons.

Pin a yo-yo centrally on the upper of one espadrille. Using a contrasting-colored thread, stitch the button to the center of the yo-yo (see page 16). Using matching thread, neatly catch the edges of the whole yo-yo onto the background fabric of the upper.

Repeat this sequence on the other shoe.

EMBROIDERED YO-YO

This is a more refined version of the large yo-yo and is adapted from the embroidered yo-yo on pages 38-41. You will need two single ribbon yo-yos (see page 37), stranded embroidery floss in a matching color, and a large embroidery needle.

Pin one small yo-yo centrally on the front of one espadrille, allowing at least 1in (2.5cm) around it for embroidery. Baste on the outside edge. Measure and mark approximately ¾in (2cm) outside the edge with a water-soluble pen. Embroider a row of basic herringbone stitch (see page 17) extending from the ribbon edge to the drawn edge. Add other ties to the herringbones, if you like, or use different colored threads. We have made two ties, vertical and horizontal, but kept to the same color.

When finished, remove the drawn line and the basting stitches. Repeat the same steps for the other shoe.

EMBROIDERED RIBBON STRIP

This simple design can be made from some left-over ribbon scraps, as you only need two short lengths to match the width of the espadrille upper. It could look very elegant or very lively depending upon the ribbon chosen and the colors used to embroider it into position.

You will need two lengths, each approximately 7in (18cm) of $^7/_8$in (2.2cm) Jacquard ribbon plus 1in (2.5cm) extra for seam allowances, together with stranded embroidery floss in two colors. Pin a length of ribbon about 1in (2.5cm) below the top of the upper and turn the raw edges under at each end. Baste in place and hem the turned ends carefully to the fabric at the join with the sole. Using four strands of embroidery floss, work a row of herringbone stitches in a contrasting color across the top edge of the ribbon, and repeat on the lower edge in another color. Add any extra decorative ties to the herringbones (see page 17). Remove the basting threads and repeat for the other shoe.

Embellished espadrilles

You can embellish your espadrilles with either ribbons or yo-yos, stitched to the uppers with either small oversewing stitches or tied herringbone stitches in harmonizing or contrasting colors.

Shirt

We couldn't resist decorating a white shirt with an adaptation of the half yo-yo band design (see pages 50-53), too. This bright and bold graphic design would look good with a favorite pair of jeans or super smart with a suit for work.

For a similar decoration to the one shown opposite, you will need six half yo-yos made with 1½-in (4-cm) wide Jacquard ribbon and two lengths of checked ribbon, each 10½ in (27cm) long, backed with fusible fabric (see page 12). You can easily alter the length of the button band decoration by adding more yo-yos to the ribbon binding, but you will need to adjust the ribbon length accordingly.

HALF YO-YO BAND

1 Place three yo-yos edge to edge on a flat surface. Pin and baste one ribbon strip onto the straight sides to hide all the raw edges. Fold the edge of the checked ribbon under at the bottom yo-yo and baste into position.

2 Place the ribbon strip about ¾in (2cm) from the edge of the shirt front or button band, making sure the ribbon can be seen when the buttons are fastened. Pin into position and fold over the top edge of the ribbon on a slant to fit against the shirt collar band.

3 Baste and top-stitch using a monofilament or matching thread [fig 1].

4 Repeat on the other side of the shirt opening, making sure that the two ribbon strips are equal. When complete, remove all basting threads.

5 Slip stitch the edges of the yo-yos to the shirt fabric using a matching thread [fig 2].

Half yo-yo buttonband

OPPOSITE This simple white shirt has a half yo-yo button band decoration that fits neatly under the collar and comes to just below bust level. The length of the band can easily be altered to suit the style of the shirt, as can the size of the half yo-yos. These were made with a wide Jacquard ribbon, but you could opt for a narrower one for a more delicate-looking version.

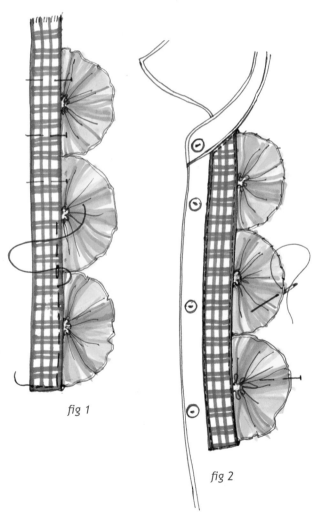

fig 1

fig 2

Hats

Everyone should have a lovely straw hat for the summer, and making different ribbon trims will take the same simple hat to many different places. Here are two designs to get you started, and you will think of many more ideas once you get the hang of the basic making method.

YO-YO FLOWERS HAT BAND

This is the simplest of the hats trims, with ribbon and buttoned yo-yo flowers. Just find the perfect ribbon for your outfit, the wider the better,

before selecting several colors and widths of grosgrain ribbon for the flowers.

You will need a length of wide Jacquard ribbon to fit the hat's circumference plus turnings, together with three double yo-yos (see page 37), each made with contrasting wide and narrow grosgrain ribbons, with decorative buttons to contrast with the yo-yo ribbons.

Wrap the wide ribbon around the hat and secure with a few basting stitches. Take the largest yo-yo and stitch it over the join in the hat

ribbon, incorporating the button as you stitch (see page 16)—this will hold the yo-yo in place. Arrange the other two yo-yos so that they slightly overlap one another and the large yo-yo, and stitch buttons to the centers.

YO-YO RIBBON BOW HAT BAND

Check that the spacing of the yo-yos will work out—this depends on the size of your hat and how closely spaced you want the yo-yos.

You will need your chosen number of small yo-yos (see page 37) made with $^7/_8$-in (2.2-cm) wide Jacquard ribbons, and a matching number of different size 2- or 4-hole buttons in colors that blend. You also need 1 yd (1m) of narrow $^1/_2$-in (1.2-cm) lightweight checked ribbon for the hat band, and a bodkin or large-eyed blunt needle (for threading the ribbons).

Thread the needle with the ribbon and pull it through the hole of the first yo-yo, and pull the yo-yo to the far end of the ribbon, leaving a long tail free to tie into a bow later. Pass the ribbon through holes of the button (and then through the other two holes with a 4-hole button to form a cross) before taking it back through the hole of the yo-yo to secure the button in place. Position the next yo-yo, and repeat at equal spacings until all yo-yos are threaded.

Tie the ribbon around the hat, arranging the yo-yos neatly. Tie a bow, leaving long streamers at the side of the hat.

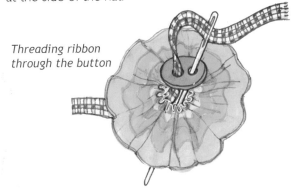

Threading ribbon through the button

Yo-yo flowers hat band
OPPOSITE The three double yo-yos have been attached to a Jacquard ribbon hat band on a summer straw hat.

Yo-yo ribbon bow hat band
LEFT Single yo-yos have been attached to a narrow gingham ribbon, which is threaded through the button embellishment of each yo-yo.

Beads

We made these beads from the ribbon scraps left over after making the ribbon fabrics for the designs, as they were too beautiful to waste. We used the backs of some of the Jacquard ribbons as they are equally lovely. You will need some scraps of felt and some leftover scraps of ribbon for the beads below plus some seed beads and metallic thread for the embellished beads shown below right. Thread the beads (combined with glass ones) onto narrow ribbons for bracelets and necklaces.

MAKING BEADS

For the beads made from ribbon and/or felt:

1 Cut a piece of colored felt to the same width as the chosen ribbon, about 4–6in (10–15cm) long. Wrap the felt around a narrow knitting needle or wooden skewer and secure the end in place with a few stitches [fig 1].

2 Continue to wrap the felt and when at the desired size, overstitch the end to secure [fig 2].

3 Take a small length of ribbon that will wrap around the felt base. Stitch the end to the felt with embroidery floss [fig 3].

4 Wrap the ribbon around once and turn under the raw edge. Using embroidery floss oversew the top and base of each bead so the layers stay in place [fig 4]. Remove from the needle.

For the embellished beads using a felt or ribbon backing:

5 Using metallic thread, wrap the felt bead with the thread [fig 5].

6 Thread the seed beads onto embroidery floss, then stitch through the woven backs of the ribbon bead so they are randomly spaced [fig 6].

7 Finish the top and bottom edges of the beads with rows of colored beads [fig 7].

Mixed bead necklace

OPPOSITE Mixed handmade ribbon beads with some glass beads create a colorful necklace, threaded on ribbon.

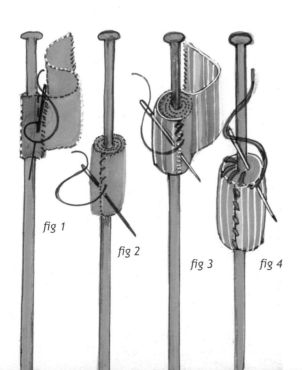

fig 1 *fig 2* *fig 3* *fig 4*

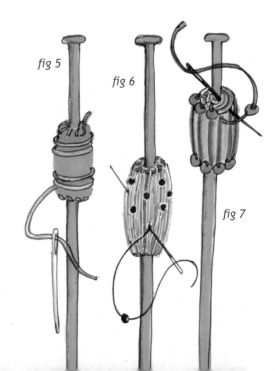

fig 5 *fig 6* *fig 7*

Templates

The templates shown on the following pages are all shown at 50 percent of actual size. To recreate each one at actual size, photocopy it at 200 percent.

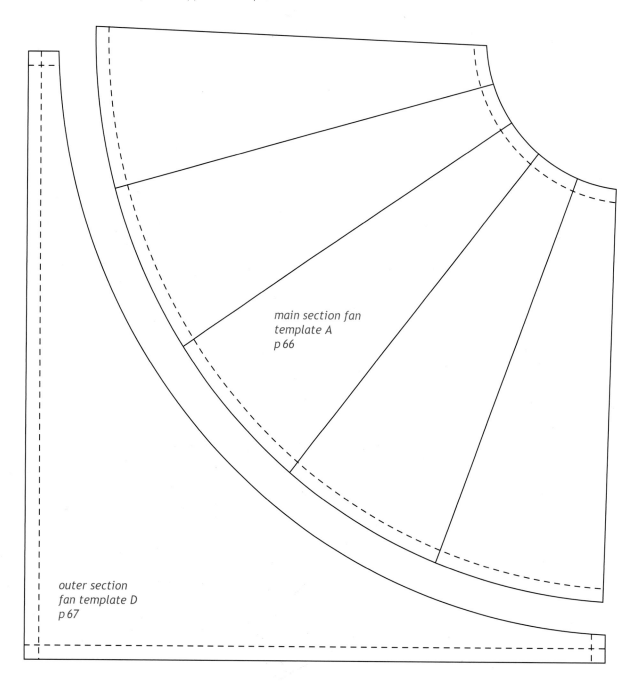

main section fan template A p 66

outer section fan template D p 67

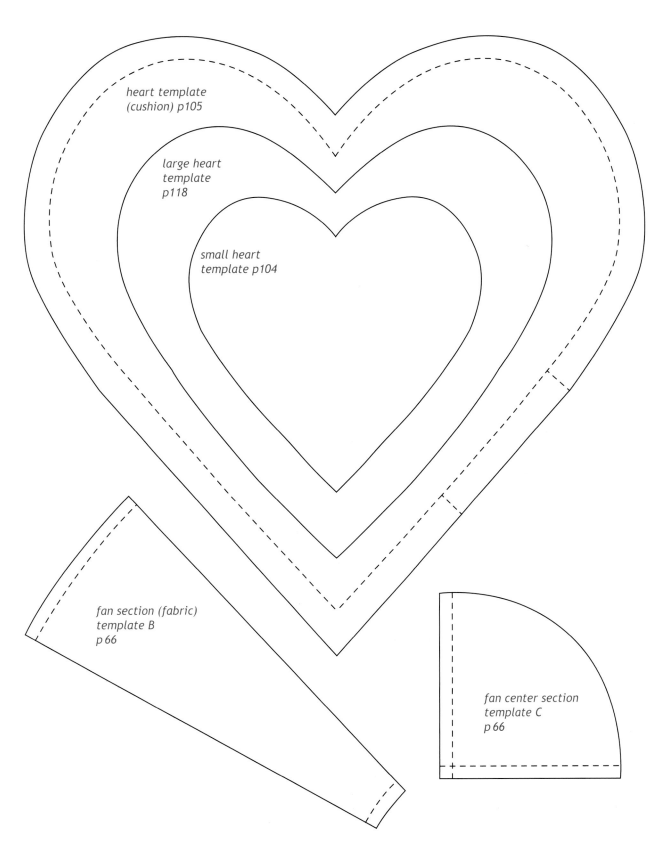

heart template
(cushion) p105

large heart
template
p118

small heart
template p104

fan section (fabric)
template B
p 66

fan center section
template C
p 66

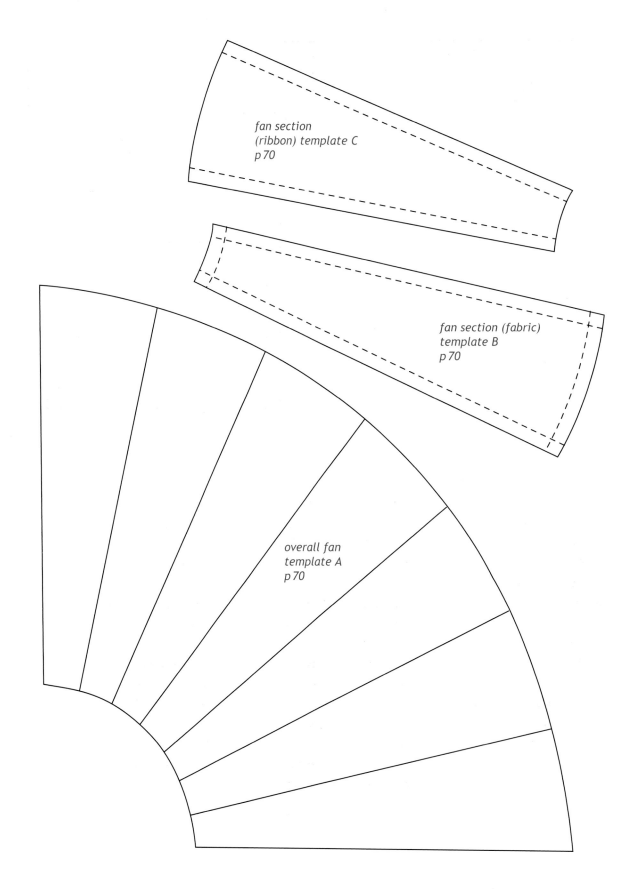

fan section
(ribbon) template C
p 70

fan section (fabric)
template B
p 70

overall fan
template A
p 70

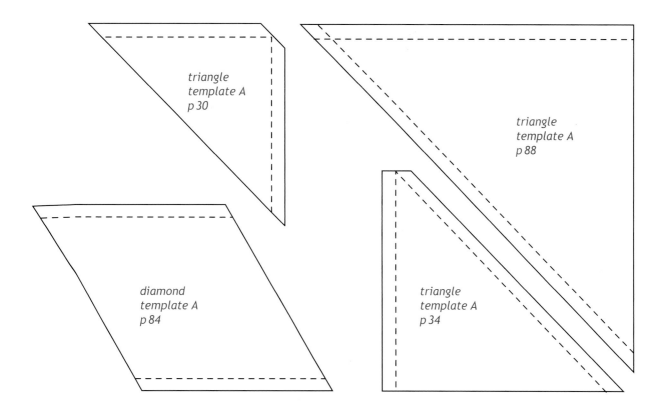

triangle template A p 30

triangle template A p 88

diamond template A p 84

triangle template A p 34

SOURCES

USA

Glorious Color Inc
(KF ribbons and fabrics)
Box 205, Solebury
PA 18963-0205
contact@gloriouscolor.com
www.gloriouscolor.com

Renaissance Ribbons
(KF ribbons and grosgrains)
9690 Stackhouse Lane
Oregon House CA 95962
www.renaissanceribbons.com
info@RenaissanceRibbons.com

UK

The Cotton Patch
(KF ribbons and fabrics)
1283-1285 Stratford Road,
Hall Green, Birmingham
B28 9AJ
mailorder@cottonpatch.co.uk
www.cottonpatch.co.uk

Lady Sew and Sew
(KF ribbons and fabrics)
Farm Road
Henley-on-Thames
Oxon, RG9 1EJ
info@ladysewandsew.co.uk
www.ladysewandsew.co.uk

Whaleys (Bradford Ltd)
(fusible fabrics and web)
Harris Court, Great Horton,
Bradford, West Yorkshire
BD7 4EQ
info@whaleysltd.co.uk
www.whaleys-bradford.ltd.uk

The Scotland Shop
(tartan ribbons)
Greenknowe, Duns,
Berwickshire TD11 3JA
info@scotlandshop.com
www.scotlandshop.com

MAKING AN ENVELOPE CUSHION COVER

You need to measure your sample and/or decide on the dimensions of the cover front. You will need a piece of fabric three times the size of the sample to make the front and two back pieces.

1 Measure the sample/determine the size of the front cover, add ¼in (6mm) to each side. Cut out.

2 Cut out two pieces of backing fabric each half the size of the front, plus 6in (15cm), plus the usual allowances and add a further ½in (1.2cm) to each piece to create the overlapped opening [fig 1].

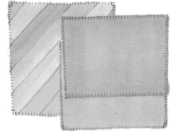

fig 1

3 Then fold over twice the opening edge of each piece of backing fabric to form a hem, and pin in position. Machine stitch each hem in place.

4 Lay the cushion front WS down. Place one backing piece WS down on top, lining up outer edges, and place the other piece on top, also WS down, lining up outer edges again and pin [fig 2]. Machine stitch around all the edges. Turn right sides out.

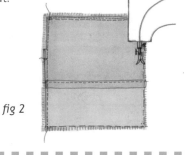

fig 2

AUTHORS' ACKNOWLEDGMENTS

Our heartfelt thanks go to many people who have helped to bring this book to publication: first and foremost to **Susan Berry** of Berry & Co, who first suggested that we look at Kaffe Fassett's ribbons, to see if we could design some interesting things for people to make with them.

Thanks also to **Edith Minne** at Renaissance Ribbons for her enthusiastic response to the initial designs and her generosity in providing many of the beautiful Jacquard ribbons and to her assistant who promptly sent us everything we asked for, and more; to **Nik Sewell**, the owner of The Cotton Patch, and **Beth Sheard**, Kaffe's former assistant, our grateful thanks for their efficiency and helpfulness in providing materials. To **Steven Wooster** for his simple and stylish photography and layouts, and to **Katie Hardwicke**, who carefully and kindly steered me through the final editing process.

Thanks, of course, to the staff team at Heart Space: **Ilaria Padovani**, **Ceema McDowell**, **Helen Cobby**, and **Paula New**; and to **June Baker-Atkinson**, who kindly found the time to make several of the ribbon projects.

Last, but not least, to **Kaffe Fassett**, whose colorful and handsome ribbons were the inspiration behind the entire book and for his generosity writing the foreword and supplying ribbons from his own studio.

PUBLISHER'S ACKNOWLEDGMENTS

Grateful thanks to the team of people who helped to put the book together but particular thanks to **Janet Haigh**, the owner of Heart Space Studios, whose designing, making, and illustrating skills are matched only by her energy and enthusiasm.